MW01007546

School Rethink 2.0

School Rethink 2.0

Putting Reinvention into Practice

Edited by

Frederick M. Hess
Michael B. Horn
Juliet Squire

HARVARD EDUCATION PRESS
CAMBRIDGE, MASSACHUSETTS

Copyright © 2025 by the President and Fellows of Harvard College

All rights reserved. No part of this publication may be reproduced or transmitted in any form or by any means, electronic or mechanical, including photocopy, recording, or any information storage and retrieval systems, without permission in writing from the publisher.

Paperback ISBN 9781682539408

Library of Congress Cataloging-in-Publication Data is on file.

Published by Harvard Education Press,
an imprint of the Harvard Education Publishing Group

Harvard Education Press
8 Story Street
Cambridge, MA 02138

Cover Design: Jackie Shepard
Cover Image: Sumners/Shutterstock; Tik tak/Shutterstock

The typeface in this book is Minion Pro.

Contents

Introduction

Frederick M. Hess, Michael B. Horn,
and Juliet Squire

It's no great revelation to observe that COVID-19 turned American education upside down. It's also not new to note that the impact on students, schools, and communities has prompted parents and educators to begin rethinking much that's long been taken for granted. And policymakers and education pundits alike have made the case that meeting today's needs and tomorrow's challenges requires questioning old assumptions and erecting new models.

Unfortunately, as with many calls to overhaul schooling, there's been a lot of encouragement but far less in the way of practical advice. Promising ideas seem to work in one school but not another. "What does new thinking on the role of teachers mean for my school?," educators ask. A call to overthrow standardized lessons in favor of personalization and mastery may sound nice, but what does implementation look like given the grammar of schooling that has persisted for decades? Expanding options to include new models of learning sounds promising, but how long will they last?

These aren't easy questions. But, easy or not, they demand real-life answers.

In the aftermath of the pandemic, amid concerns about learning loss, students' social and emotional well-being, chronic absenteeism, classroom disorder, and the end of emergency school aid, there is a hunger—and an opportunity—to revisit the routines that organize and undergird school-ing. The return to business as usual has felt comforting in certain respects. Indeed, it can be a relief after the flood of well-meaning but frustratingly high-level advice regarding all the things schools could and should do differently.

Whatever the appeal of normalcy, however, parents, practitioners, and policymakers have seen that current routines aren't getting the job done. The need for schools to do better has become difficult to dismiss. From the long overdue science-of-reading push to the exodus of millions of parents and students from traditional district schools for alternative options, the results are easy to see.

Enrollment in traditional public school districts has declined precipi-tously, which suggests parents are hungry for something different.[1] The lion's share of this decline was driven not by dropouts or parents delaying kindergarten a year but by students and families opting for charter, private, and homeschool options because of issues regarding academic quality and safety.[2] More students and families have also sought out virtual schools and microschools. It's become routine for the media to note that these shifts are outlasting the pandemic.[3]

The surging interest in providing public dollars to support education choice is indicative of policymakers' frustration with old routines. In states where these policies exist, families are flocking to the learning ex-periences of their own choosing. In Florida, nearly half of students enroll outside of their zoned, traditional district option.[4] A growing number of states have adopted education savings accounts (ESAs), an approach to school choice that's proved broadly popular with voters across the ideo-logical spectrum (even though familiar left–right divisions continue when it comes to elected officials). Such results do not suggest that parents and voters are dissatisfied with traditional district schools per se; it's that they want different supports, curricula, schedules, and choices, among other things, to help educate their children.[5]

It's not just policymakers and parents who are frustrated with the sta-tus quo. The same is true of many educators. Two-thirds of teachers re-port feeling that they have little control or influence over their schools' policies.[6] According to the RAND Corporation's 2023 State of the American Teacher Survey, 23 percent of American teachers said that they were "likely to leave their job by the end of the 2022–2023 school year." And 26 percent of teachers feared for their physical safety at school, especially due to student misbehavior and verbal altercations.[7] During and after the pandemic, thousands of teachers left their traditional schools to launch new models. Indeed, the National Microschooling Center reports that two-thirds of lead instructors or founders of microschools are currently or formerly licensed educators.[8]

School leaders acutely feel the struggles of this era. Whether it's the inadequacy of the standard prescriptions to "catch students up," burnout among teachers, or the apparent anger of community members who show up at school board meetings, leaders are hungry for solutions that can help them break out of the bind.

And everyone is frustrated with how students have fared in the shadow of the pandemic. Assessment data suggest that average public school students in grades 3 through 8 have learned a lot less than their predecessors—half a year less in math and a quarter of a year less in reading.[9] When it comes to social skills and emotional maturity, 80 percent of educators report that students who suffered through the pandemic are worse off than their predecessors.[10] Whereas roughly 60 percent of Americans rated their local public schools an A or B in 2019, now only half do. As for the nation's schools as a whole, only a fifth of the general public gives them an A or B.[11]

It's a grim litany. But the challenges have also opened up an opportunity to improve schools that weren't working all that well before the pandemic either. Declining National Assessment of Educational Progress scores, disengaged students, abysmal career and technical education (CTE), and a frustrated teaching workforce all painted a portrait of discontent even before 2020. The challenge was that in a system as big, familiar, and routinized as US K–12 education, it was hard for that kind of discontent to lead to reflection, much less meaningful change.

The pandemic acted as a giant pause button by putting those routines on hold while forcing individual families and educators to break old habits and settle into new ones. Things that had long been familiar suddenly got a fresh look. The result was a budding sense that rethinking was not only possible but also necessary—and that reopening schools wasn't nearly enough. What was needed was a more fundamental reinvention.

Despite all this dislocation and dissatisfaction, as the pandemic has receded, the traditional routines and rhythms of schooling have gradually reasserted themselves (even if some of those, such as the expectation that students will be in school every day, are less evident than they once were). If educators don't act now, it's likely that the moment will pass. It will be all too easy for inertia to take hold, with too many students and families consigned to unsatisfactory arrangements when it comes to what gets taught and how, where and when education happens, how students experience schooling, and how schools are staffed.

Against that backdrop, many have sketched aspirational, high-level visions for reassembling schooling. That includes the editors of this volume. Between the three of us, we've spent more than a half century in the weeds of educational improvement and transformation in terms of governance, staffing, technology, leadership, and much else. Since the pandemic hit, Michael authored *From Reopen to Reinvent*.[12] Rick penned *The Great School Rethink*.[13] And Julie is the force behind Bellwether's highly regarded Assembly initiative.[14] We've each offered frameworks for rethinking how schooling is done, provided advice and tips for educators of all stripes to put this into practice, and identified what schools might do differently. We believe such efforts have a useful role to play in helping expand our notion of how schools might work and what it'll take to deliver for our kids.

But much more is needed to seize the opportunity before it disappears. Above all, what's lacking is the dissemination of concrete, on-the-ground wisdom regarding what to do and how to do it. That's where this book comes in.

RETHINKING IN PRACTICE

There are a lot of ways we might try to reinvent schooling. There are fundamental changes to the existing system. There are new providers of new models within and outside that system. There are new classroom practices enabled by new roles for adults and technology. We three have studied, supported, and written about these efforts at length. But reinventing education isn't ultimately about abstractions and theories of change. It's about the practical actions that educators, parents, and policymakers take to put them into practice.

After all, it's not like "reforming schools" is a new idea. Arguably, American school reform is as old as American schooling itself—dating back at least to Thomas Jefferson, Benjamin Rush, and other founders who offered sweeping visions of how to ensure that the new nation's schools would educate the citizens it required for its success. Over the course of time, this reform impulse has yielded a now-familiar seesawing between competing visions of change. Many years ago, in *Tinkering Toward Utopia*, historians David Tyack and Larry Cuban observed that reforms come and go. Calls for centralization are frequently followed by those for decentralization. Desires for heightened attention to academics inevitably give rise to demands for more focus on practical knowledge or career education.[15]

Schools and educators get bombarded by waves of proposed change. The result is a culture of "spinning wheels" in which veteran educators have learned to wait out each new wave while wearily reassuring each other, "This too shall pass."[16] The constant wash of reform makes it tough for any proposal to stick or be taken seriously.

Even frustrated educators and communities can be justifiably leery when they hear talk of rethinking or reinvention. The idea in question may be unfamiliar and sound more like edu-babble than a practical solution. Parents may be reluctant to embrace something when it's unclear how or whether it actually works. Policymakers may find a proposal intriguing but be unsure what it entails or how to keep it from going off the rails. Moreover, any veteran of reform efforts may be justifiably cynical about pushes to overhaul education. It's easy to look askance at calls for fundamental change when the history of education reform is saturated with disappointing innovations and short-lived reforms.

We understand and appreciate this hesitation. Frankly, we get pretty nervous when we encounter education leaders who are eager to immediately jump on the latest bandwagon.

Part of the challenge is to ask whether we can do better this time around.

We've found that perhaps the most promising way to address educators' concerns is to let them see things up close, warts and all. Superintendents, principals, and teachers should have an opportunity to get beyond the spin and ask hard questions, kick the tires, and get a sense of what it actually takes for reinvention to deliver.

That's what this book is about. We've tried to recruit a bunch of the smartest, most thoughtful, and most experienced *doers* we know to talk about the practical work of reinvention.

Notice that we said "doers." The contributors to this volume are individuals who've spent an extraordinary amount of time getting their hands dirty with the messy work of rethinking schools and the practical challenges of reinventing them. Most of them have few opportunities to write, relate their experiences, or share the lessons they've learned— precisely because they're busy leading the work in the field.

Our goal is to provide a clear window into what it looks like to reinvent schooling with no spin and as little varnish as possible. We've asked the contributors to talk about the challenges they're tackling and the opportunities they see but also the stumbles, impediments, and frustrations they've dealt with. You'll encounter an array of voices, including those working on technology, assessment, CTE, and staffing, as well as those collaborating with educators and families outside of district schools to rethink dimensions like school size, school financing, and the extent of education choice. The aim is to provide a practical sense of the possibilities, the pitfalls, and the intangible qualities that it takes to ensure that rethinking born in the crisis of the pandemic isn't one more case of ambitious theorizing that disappoints in practice.

We don't for a moment imagine that any specific effort in this volume is the one your school or system needs to embrace. And we don't want anyone to assume that the inclusion of an author or organization here means we're recommending or endorsing them. We've brought these contributors together not because of their esoteric musings but because they're seasoned, sensible authorities with insight into what this work actually involves. Their collective tenure in education is measured in decades, and they span a variety of roles.

We're also not holding up what follows as a litany of prescriptive best practices. For starters, we tend to think that "best practices" is the sort of phrase that gets thrown about far too casually in education. It conveys the idea that there is one best way to accomplish a task. In reality, best practices are defined by circumstances, students, available resources, priorities, and much else.

These contributors aren't just providing examples of where their specific approach has worked. Rather, they're detailing how they defined the problem they were trying to solve, what their mindset was when they built their solution, and how to know when their solution might be the right fit. In other words, what are the conditions under which their models make sense for you—and what are the larger lessons you can take away from their successes and failures?

THE BOOK AHEAD

We want to be clear about how we selected our contributors: we chose them precisely because they're *not* cheerleaders or self-promoters. We asked them to make time for this work because we find them to be straight shooters who, over a cup of coffee or a couple of beers, can share stories that can be both eye-opening and hugely instructive to those of us who aren't in the rooms or on the Zooms they inhabit. We wanted to give you the same kind of straight-from-the-shoulder tutorial they've given us that we've found so instructive on so many occasions.

We asked contributors to grapple with some big questions: What's the problem that they've been trying to solve? Why have they gravitated toward specific solutions? What does their work really look like on the ground? What has gotten in their way? How have they navigated those challenges? And are there places where their solution hasn't worked, but they are able to extract larger lessons for readers?

The goal was to get real about the problems and solutions and then to describe how this all plays out in practice. Our intent is to provide a real look at what it takes to rethink or reinvent schooling—not just in a seminar or PowerPoint presentation but in real communities and on the ground.

The book covers everything from the trendy themes of artificial intelligence (AI) and CTE to the eternal questions of what we teach and how we assess student learning. The first section grapples with how schools can personalize learning, with chapters from Khan Academy's Sal Khan, Kristen DiCerbo, and Rachel Boroditsky on AI; MasteryTrack CEO and founder Scott Ellis on mastery learning; and The Learning Accelerator CEO Beth Rabbitt on personalization. The second set focuses on rethinking the structure of schools, containing chapters written by Brent W. Maddin, executive director of the Next Education Workforce, an initiative of the Mary Lou Fulton Teachers College at Arizona State University, on restructuring the teaching job; Stand Together Trust senior director, Adam Peshek, on the proliferation of education choice; and EdChoice's director of national research, Michael Q. McShane, on microschools. The final group tackles efforts to rethink curriculum, instruction, and assessment, and has chapters written by the Center for Advanced Professional Studies (CAPS) Network president and executive director, Corey Mohn, on CTE; New Classrooms CEO and cofounder, Joel Rose, on rethinking math; New Meridian founder and CEO, Arthur VanderVeen, on assessment; and Amplify CEO, Larry Berger, and chief product officer, Alexandra Walsh, on curriculum.

Chapter 1 dives into the world of AI's much-hyped and -feared presence in education. Through the experience of Sal Khan, founder of Khan Academy; Kristen DiCerbo, Khan Academy's chief learning officer; and Rachel Boroditsky, Khan Academy's chief of staff, we learn about the creation of Khanmigo—Khan Academy's AI tutor—and how it's been implemented in different schools, as well as the challenges they've faced. Although schools have had polar-opposite reactions to AI (some have banned its use while others have excitedly embraced it), Sal, Kristen, and Rachel discuss generative AI's capabilities, how schools can better harness its promise, concerns about privacy and academic dishonesty, and how schools might balance competing priorities when it comes to AI.

Chapter 2 explores how to implement mastery learning, also known as competency-based education. Scott Ellis—the founder and CEO of Mastery-Track, a free software platform that offers a structure for implementing mastery learning—explains the tenets of mastery learning and shows how it upends many of the assumptions underpinning traditional schooling. Competency-based education rejects conventional notions of seat time in favor of an approach in which students only progress once they've shown mastery of a particular concept. Although mastery learning enjoys widespread appeal and attention—see, for example, the Educational Testing Service and the Carnegie Foundation's high-profile joint effort to move in its direction—there's considerable confusion about how mastery learning can be implemented, its impact on grading and pacing, and what problems it solves versus what questions it raises. Scott shares how he has navigated these practical questions in a variety of schools and classrooms, as he grappled with them when working with educators in subjects ranging from social studies and math to learning guitar and tennis. Scott paints a picture of what mastery learning can look like in diverse settings and discusses the lessons he's learned and pitfalls he's encountered while implementing it.

Chapter 3 explores personalization. Since COVID-19, there's been a rush to tutoring to help get students back on track, based on the theory that greater personalization is the best way for students to learn. And yet, so many of these tutoring efforts have disappointed in practice. In this chapter, Beth Rabbitt, CEO of The Learning Accelerator, distills some of the core lessons we've learned from past efforts to replace one-size-fits-all models of instruction with greater personalization. This trend, in other words, isn't new—nor are the disappointments. (The efforts to differentiate instruction in the 1990s and 2000s and the rush to use education technology in the 2010s come to mind here.) In this chapter, Beth draws on her work at The Learning Accelerator, where she supports a wide array of schools and systems in distilling actionable lessons around efforts to personalize learning. She explains some of the features of personalization that are consistent across successful models, describes the conditions that allow personalization to take root, and argues that the *why* of personalization is just as important as the *what* and the *how*. She concludes with a set of concrete takeaways for rethinking practice and policy that are designed to help personalization deliver on its promise.

Chapter 4 focuses on rethinking the structure of teaching and learning itself. It begins by addressing the elephant in the room: that team-based teaching is not a new approach. Brent Maddin, executive director of the

Next Education Workforce at Arizona State University, explains how societal forces, robust research, technology (including AI), and keen interest among influential education organizations may provide the conditions to make team-based teaching succeed where it had previously failed to take root. He then sketches the principles of an alternative teaching model that leverages teams of educators with distributed expertise. Brent also dives into the specifics: what it means to do this in schools; the challenges implicit in existing training; how to work through traditional staffing rules, collective bargaining agreements, and teacher-of-record requirements; and the implications of all this for policy and practice.

Chapter 5 delves into the burgeoning landscape of education choices for students. Debates in education often pit school choice and voucher programs against traditional public school districts. But new forms of choice, powered by ESAs, are allowing families to use public dollars to choose a variety of options. Adam Peshek, senior director and senior fellow at Stand Together Trust, has extensive experience in developing and advocating for policies that expand educational options. In this chapter, he takes us through what ESAs are and how they might change the partnership between educators and parents in a mutually beneficial way. Adam describes how parents and educators are responding to new possibilities and what perils lurk in these new and more ambitious systems, and he offers six lessons for those seeking to expand education choice through public policy while working with a coalition of stakeholders who may have different goals.

Chapter 6 builds on the theme of changing the structures of schools themselves by looking at the growing momentum behind smaller, more intimate schooling experiences. Michael McShane, director of national research at EdChoice, details EdChoice's polling on hybrid homeschooling and other school models. After the pandemic, it's perhaps no surprise to see a spike in interest in models like microschools, tutoring, and learning pods. It's clear, then, that many families are rethinking their prior beliefs about what a school looks like. Michael discusses the implications of this shift and helps educators understand the costs and benefits of small-scale schooling, how microschools and hybrid homeschooling can work in practice, and the challenges that arise.

Chapter 7 ushers in the final section of the book, which focuses on what schools teach. In recent years, there's been a renaissance in CTE options in schools. Corey Mohn—president and executive director of the CAPS Network, which seeks to smooth the education-to-employment path through profession-based learning using partnerships between local industries and school districts—explains what it looks like to offer CTE in the twenty-first century through real-world business projects and the development of professional skills. Corey describes how CAPS got its start in a Kansas suburb and explains how students and community members interact with one another in the experimental school district. He then applies his lessons to the building of a movement more generally and offers advice to those seeking to channel energy to enact bold change in education, as well as making clear the challenges and risks involved in doing so.

Chapter 8 explains how we might rethink math instruction. In this chapter, Joel Rose, cofounder and CEO of New Classrooms Innovation Partners—a company that works with more than one hundred schools across the nation to deliver a new model of math learning—advocates leveraging technology to offer students greater personalization and discusses how the New Classrooms model can help struggling math students catch up with their on-grade-level peers. Joel draws on many of the prior chapters in this book—especially those on team-based teaching, mastery learning, and personalization—to describe both the opportunities for rethinking math instruction and the different roadblocks in implementation. Joel addresses challenges from pacing to assessment and explains how New Classrooms has sought to work through those obstacles during implementation.

Chapter 9 takes readers on a deep dive into assessments. Arthur VanderVeen is the founder and CEO of New Meridian, which designs and develops standardized assessments that emphasize critical thinking, problem solving, and effective communication—and, most importantly, that are designed to *help students learn* rather than simply *measure what they have learned*. On the heels of decades of debate about high-stakes assessments, Arthur argues that there's a clear need for reliable assessments that serve both families and educators. This chapter begins by explaining why our current assessments fall short and goes on to detail three design principles that rethinkers should consider when developing a student-first approach to assessment for learning. Throughout the chapter, Arthur details how New Meridian has dealt with the challenges of rethinking assessment and argues that reliable assessments should provide real-time feedback to teachers, who can then use these data to help students learn throughout the year.

Chapter 10 delivers a primer on curriculum itself. Larry Berger is the founder and CEO of Amplify, an industry leader in next-generation curriculum and formative assessments that serves fifteen million students. In this chapter, he and his colleague Alexandra Walsh, chief product officer at Amplify, lay out nine barriers to innovation in the core textbook and curriculum markets that are all too often overlooked. After outlining the challenges, Larry and Alexandra conclude with reasons for hope, including the budding desire for high-quality instructional materials, the actions taken by visionary states, the increased availability of open education resources, and an appetite among teachers for software suites. Throughout the chapter, the authors explain why scrappy upstart curriculum companies may be better suited than the entrenched oligopoly of education publishers to take advantage of today's unique instructional needs, and they offer reflections on how educators can navigate the array of curricular choices they now encounter.

MOVING FORWARD

We've tried to craft an accessible, straightforward, and practical resource on how to tackle rethinking in education. In this book, we've tapped those who've been at the forefront of this work to gain their insights, experiences, and practical wisdom. In other words, we're trying to peel back the curtain on high-profile efforts to rethink and assemble the fundamental tenets of schooling. We hope we've compiled a practical guide to help you think through not just what you want to do but why you want to do it, the process you might follow, and where you may run into stumbling blocks.

Now it's time to roll up our sleeves and join these educators and innovators on the journey to not just rethink schools but appreciate what it takes to tackle the practical work of reinventing them.

1

Rethinking the Promise
of AI in Education

Sal Khan, Kristen DiCerbo,
and Rachel Boroditsky

In September 2022, OpenAI president Greg Brockman gave Khan Academy access to the newly trained large language model (LLM) we now know as GPT-4.[1] We spent three days asking the model to do everything from writing quiz questions about the Bill of Rights to generating ideas to get more people to use Khan Academy (and writing poems for our spouses).

Anyone who has played around on GPT-4 or its predecessor, GPT-3.5, knows that the program is great at giving users answers to any questions they ask. For our work at Khan Academy, though, we wanted the model to act as a competent tutor rather than an answer-generating machine. Our partners at OpenAI gave us our first lesson in *prompt engineering*, or writing the instructions that tell the model how to respond. They suggested we give these instructions:

> This is a dialogue between a student and an extremely qualified, kind, experienced, encouraging, patient, empathetic, and flexible tutor. The tutor always says "I don't know" if they are unsure how to respond. The tutor uses the Socratic method to help the student reflect on their answer—that is, thinking about their thinking. The tutor asks leading questions and never gives a full answer unless the student is correct. The tutor adapts the

conversation and methods to make sure the student independently learns core concepts of the topic and reasoning, not just memorizing.

This was the beginning of our crash course in generative AI.[2]

Following these first few days, we brought our team together in a hackathon to brainstorm possibilities. We soon threw out our existing roadmap of the features we were planning on building for the year and pivoted to building an AI-powered offering to launch alongside OpenAI's public release of GPT-4. In March 2023, we released Khanmigo, which is both an AI-powered tutor for students and an assistant for teachers.

Since that launch, we have had countless conversations with people across the education space; observed its use in classrooms; interviewed students, teachers, and administrators; and closely examined incoming data on interactions with Khanmigo.

We have found ourselves riding the Gartner hype cycle, going from the peak of inflated expectations and thinking this technology could do everything to the trough of disillusionment (especially after seeing some of its early math performance), and finally climbing up the slope of enlightenment as we determined how we could work with the technology.[3] We are still figuring out AI's education-based limitations, but we now have a good idea of what the technology can do and some informed guesses about what it might look like in schools in the near- to medium-term future.

THE PROBLEM

AI holds promise to tackle some of the major problems we see in education in the US, including declining student learning outcomes and teacher burnout, attrition, and shortages. These are by no means the only issues in education, but they are significant challenges that AI has real potential to help address.

Student Learning Outcomes

Recent National Assessment of Educational Progress (NAEP) scores have been a major cause for concern in education. Data from 2023 show stagnating or decreasing performance in math and reading among American students: the math comprehension of an average thirteen-year-old has

fallen to levels comparable to those of the 1990s, while scores for readers look more like those from 1971. NAEP's long-term trend assessments
reveal that performance started decreasing even before the pandemic, but
the most significant drops have occurred since 2020.[4] Additionally, NAEP
proficiency rates for both math and reading have highlighted significant
disparities among students from different socioeconomic, racial, and eth-
nic backgrounds—gaps that have only widened over the last few years.

Teacher Burnout, Attrition, and Shortages

Unfortunately, at a time when student needs are greatest, many teachers
are hard-pressed to meet them. Teachers want to focus on providing differentiated and personalized instruction in the classroom but find themselves crunched for time due to their growing workloads and the large
number of students in their classrooms. In a recent nationally representative survey, teachers reported spending about twenty-five hours per week
on actual teaching and twenty-five hours per week on other activities, including grading, planning, and general administrative tasks.[5] In our work
with thousands of educators at Khan Academy, we consistently hear that
there are not enough hours in the day for teachers to accomplish everything on their lists. Teacher supports are often limited, leading to heightened stress and exhaustion.

Unsurprisingly, teachers are burning out and leaving their schools or
even the profession entirely. According to the Government Accountability
Office, there was a 7 percent decrease in the total teaching population, or a
reduction of 233 thousand instructors, between 2019 and 2021. However,
teacher attrition and shortages aren't felt evenly. While some states have
seen an improvement in staffing, approximately three out of four states
reported ongoing shortages, with subject matter vacancies in areas like
physical education, special education, and STEM.[6] This continues a trend
that has been getting worse over the last decade. As Gerard Robinson of
the Center for Advancing Opportunity wrote in *The 74*,

> In the 2011–2012 school year, 19 percent of public schools were unable to
> fill a teaching position for biology or life sciences. By the 2020–2021 school
> year, that number had grown to 31 percent. The situation was similar for

other subjects, going from 19 percent to 32 percent for mathematics, and 26 percent to 47 percent for physical sciences, such as physics, geology and engineering.[7]

These shortages portend a further negative impact on student learning.

AI TO THE RESCUE?

Since the advent of the computer, there has been interest in using digital technology to address education problems. Researchers have been developing tutoring systems to support student learning and automated scoring systems to ease teachers' grading burdens for decades. The emergence of generative AI in recent years has the potential to supercharge education technology as a tool for both students and teachers, helping to address learning loss and teacher burnout.

A Brief History of AI in Classrooms

First, a little history. Technologists in the 1970s began exploring how AI might help students learn under the banner of "computer-assisted instruction." Over time, intelligent tutors—educational technologies that provide personalized and adaptive instruction to learners—improved, and meta-analyses have shown that some computer-assisted instruction can have large impacts on learning.[8] More recent research suggests that digital learning and practice systems that provide students sufficient opportunities to practice a skill (at least seven opportunities per skill) result in remarkably consistent gains in learning.[9] It seems that technology-enabled learning systems that provide the right amount of practice on the right skills can and do improve students' learning outcomes.

For some teachers, the use of AI began with automated essay grading. Scoring open-ended responses is time-consuming for teachers. Technologists developed an automated essay scoring method of gathering a large sample of human-scored essays and extracting features from them (word count, average sentence length, average word length, etc.), which were then combined into a score. Over time, researchers developed techniques to understand the meaning of words and capture features like cohesion, coherence, and key concepts. Today, models can separately score different aspects of writing and produce scores that align with those that human beings give to the same essays.

The Entrance of Generative AI

Late 2022 and early 2023 brought national attention to generative AI. Generative AI refers to artificial intelligence systems that can create original data or content, such as text, images, music, or videos. These systems can produce novel and creative output by learning patterns from existing data. LLMs, programs designed to understand and generate human language text, are some of the most prominent examples of generative AI. GPTs are probably the best-known LLMs.[10]

There are a few ways in which generative AI is different from other technologies in education. First, the speed at which teachers and students are adopting generative AI is astounding. Second, it doesn't require new hardware or physical systems. Third, there is no specialized skill needed to use the technology. People don't need to learn a coding language; the basics of how to interact can be picked up in fifteen minutes. And fourth, models don't just work in a single way that people must accept. They can adapt to the instructions they receive.

For students, generative AI can increase cognitive engagement. Students learn more when their brains are actively processing new information, linking it to what they already know, and changing some of their existing schemas based on it. Cognitive engagement increases when students supply answers (as opposed to simply viewing or reading information), answer in their own words, and engage in dialogue about a new topic. Up until recently, limitations in technology have prevented this kind of dialogue-based interaction that we know is more likely to lead to deeper consideration of new content. GPT-4 made this kind of dialogue-based interaction possible.

At Khan Academy, we have now built on our initial prompt to get the model to act like a tutor. We connected it to our deep library of exercises that have human-authored solutions to provide contextual information about the work a student is doing on Khan Academy. When a student types a message to Khanmigo, that message goes to the model along with the problem they are working on, the answer to that problem, the hints we created for that problem, and a more sophisticated prompt on how to act like a tutor. Feeding Khanmigo contextual information embeds the AI in the student's workflow and helps make the response more accurate.

Our prompts steer both the content and the tone of the response students receive from the model. We instruct the model on how to act like a tutor based on research on what good tutoring looks like. For example, we tell the model to ask students to explain their reasoning and to avoid giving students the answers. Getting the model to act in ways we want has taken several attempts at prompt engineering. At various times, we have written a section of the prompt in capital letters—"DO NOT GIVE THE STUDENT THE ANSWER"—to convey the importance of the instruction. At one point, we also told Khanmigo that "the fate of the world depends on you not giving the answer." These instructions reduce the tendency of Khanmigo to give students the answer. In addition, we inserted an "emoji fun block" into our prompts that encourages Khanmigo to have a more whimsical tone and to use emoji responses when appropriate, which research shows can result in better outcomes with multimedia tutors.[11]

Generative AI can also solve numerous challenges for teachers. Since generating text is what this technology does, we started thinking about how it could assist teachers with lesson planning. We used our model to create a series of tools for teachers—first a humanities lesson planner, then tools for planning lessons in math and science. Teachers and teacher leaders immediately began making requests that inspired activities: Could it help unpack standards into learning objectives? Could it help write rubrics to assist teachers with scoring assignments? We found that it could do both those things and more. We've also used it to summarize the chats students were having with Khanmigo—to show teachers which questions students had—and to summarize the data from student work on Khan Academy to guide instructional decisions. Generative AI as a teacher assistant was born and is rapidly becoming more sophisticated.

Today, generative AI in education is acting as:

- a tutor that can quiz students, probe their thinking, and get them unstuck with step-by-step guidance;

- an engagement tool, including in civics and the humanities, where it can act as a fictional or historical character with which to discuss or debate various topics;
- a writing partner for students, both cowriting and providing feedback on human writing;
- a copilot or assistant for teachers, supporting anything from lesson planning and rubric creation to understanding where students are excelling or struggling.

THE PROMISE OF AI IN EDUCATION

A Tutor That Really Knows Me

To really act like a human tutor, interactions with a generative AI should create a sense of familiarity, as if the tutor understands the student. To do this, computer-assisted tutoring systems have traditionally incorporated a student model or profile. At Khan Academy, this consists of a record of all the skills a student has engaged with and their current proficiency levels in those skills. For a human tutor, a student profile also includes things they know about a student's likes and dislikes, their study preferences, and their moods.

Imagine you are a student who has been interacting with a generative AI tutor. The AI stores a record of your level of proficiency on all the skills in a course, and you have informed it of your passion for soccer. As you work on a problem on, say, probabilities, the tutor notes your knowledge of probabilities and your interest in soccer. The AI then provides extra support for solving the problem, including supplying steps and explanations, and seamlessly tailors the problem to revolve around the likelihood of your favorite team winning the World Cup.

Similarly, imagine that you have mastered fractions but question their utility. Imagine further that you have told a generative AI tutor that you aspire to become a veterinarian. The next time you are faced with a fractions problem and question its practicality, your tutor might illustrate how understanding fractions relates to adjusting medical dosages to treat dogs of different sizes and give you a challenging problem in that context. Today, Khanmigo can adapt the problem to your interests and skill mastery within a single interaction. Our goal is to get generative AI to "remember" these conversations as part of a comprehensive student profile.

Let Teachers Do What Teachers Do Best

AI also holds promise for teachers. By easing the administrative and preparation burdens teachers experience daily, AI can help them focus on what matters most: differentiating instruction for and building relationships with students. With generative AI, teachers can have an assistant at their fingertips to support a wide range of tasks, from creating a lesson plan to providing a clear snapshot of how every child in their classroom is progressing. Teachers can then be better prepared to adapt their instruction—for those who would benefit from accelerated instruction or for those who need help filling in gaps, for example—and may also have more capacity to focus on building core foundational skills, addressing students' emotional well-being, and fostering a positive learning environment.

As we pilot Khanmigo in classrooms in public schools across the US, we are focusing on helping teachers save time and enabling them to do what they do best. A classroom with AI student tools should not consist of rows of students sitting by themselves wearing headphones and answering problems for hours. Teachers should still be doing things like designing and facilitating cooperative learning, working with students in small groups, and ensuring students know there is a human who cares about their learning progress.

We're seeing numerous examples of Khanmigo easing the administrative and preparation burden on teachers. In one Midwestern school district, teachers used our rubric creation tool to standardize the formatting of their rubrics. Before, teachers manually created rubrics for a new curriculum, and interventionists and administrators struggled to interpret rubrics from different classes. The teachers worked with Khanmigo to align rubrics quickly and efficiently by entering the existing standards and assignment descriptions into our rubric tool. A teacher said of this experience: "[What] used to take us three days to do, we were doing in one."

We can see how these use cases for students and teachers come together to support different classroom implementation models. For example, AI can help facilitate a center-based classroom model in which students are broken into small groups and rotate through centers. One center might involve independent skill practice using an AI-based tutor. Another center might have the teacher working with a group of students on an application activity. A third might have students engaged in cooperative learning. Teachers often spend time searching for and tailoring these kinds of learning activities to their students. In this way, the AI is augmenting the teacher, which allows them to better engage with their students.

CHALLENGES AND RISKS OF AI IN EDUCATION

There are two categories of challenges in realizing the potential of AI in education. First, there are challenges around the adoption of new technologies in education generally, including resistance to change and the digital divide. Second, there are challenges specific to generative AI, including its accuracy, potential for bias, and ability to address bad behavior from students.

Challenges Related to New Technologies

Resistance to change

Education in general is resistant to change, as seen by the laundry list of interventions and technologies that have failed to transform classrooms.[12] (As people said in the 1960s: "There is a television in every home—surely we can use that to educate every child!") In many ways, it makes sense for education to resist change. Since education is so fundamental to our society, we would not want teaching and learning to be constantly changing on a whim. However, education's resistance to change also means that promising interventions meet resistance to adoption.

For instance, in 2013, the National Council of Teachers of English came out strongly against the use of automated essay scoring on end-of-year tests. They said, in part, "Computers are unable to recognize and judge those elements that we most associate with good writing. . . . Using computers to 'read' and evaluate students' writing (1) denies students the chance to have anything but limited features recognized in their writing; and (2) compels teachers to ignore what is most important in writing instruction in order to teach what is least important."[13] More than a decade later, despite consistent evidence that AI model scoring correlates to human scoring at the same level that human beings correlate with human scoring, there is no evidence that they have changed this stance.[14]

We also don't see intelligent tutors being used consistently in classrooms. While we know that learners who spend at least thirty minutes per week using Khan Academy's MAP Accelerator see 26 to 38 percent greater-than-expected gains on standardized tests, only about 10 percent of users spend that much time on Khan Academy math content.[15] Patterns of usage of educational technology tools generally show that tools aimed at engaging learners have seen increases in use over the past two to three years. It may be that to gain adoption, intelligent tutors need to also help solve the engagement problem.

There are a variety of underlying factors that likely contribute to education's resistance to adopting helpful technology, including poor communication, types of evidence that influence teachers' decisions, beliefs about the role of technology and teachers, and inertia. (For what it's worth, we find that teachers and school leaders are most influenced by what their peers report has worked for them, rather than by efficacy evidence.) In addition, many teachers view providing feedback on writing and making choices about what students should do next as fundamental to their role as teachers. When technology takes over these roles, it conflicts with and threatens their job and identity. Incorporating generative AI in classrooms will face these same challenges. So, it is likely that even if generative AI tools were perfect (which they are not), they would still face challenges in adoption.

The digital divide

The advent of computers and the internet brought the first digital divide, where students in wealthier communities had more access to technology at younger ages, which set them up for better future opportunities.[16] We generally know what needs to be done to close this gap: get computers and internet technology into more hands through a combination of money and willpower. However, we could open a new divide if AI tools end up in the hands of wealthier learners and not those of the less fortunate. Students with access to AI would get the benefit of extra help and experience with tools that will likely be part of many jobs moving forward. Moreover, given teacher shortages, those in more privileged positions may get the technology and teachers to help them succeed, while those in underresourced communities might get just the technology.[17] This is an obvious potential problem that we can avoid. From our very first efforts to incorporate AI tools into education, we should be marshaling resources to ensure they get into historically underresourced schools.

Challenges Related to Generative AI

When we first started testing GPT-4 in 2022, we saw its potentially transformative power and knew we needed a set of norms that would help us evaluate the risks and challenges of AI tools as they developed. We adopted nine core tenets on the ethical use of AI from the Institute for Ethical AI in Education.[18] In early 2023, we used the National Institute of Standards and Technology AI Risk Mitigation Framework to expand our tenets to identify risks and ways to mitigate them.[19] We have not eliminated all risks, but we share our approach as an example of the importance of thinking through solutions that substantially reduce the risks involved with learners interacting with AI.

Ensuring accuracy

Response accuracy, specifically in math, is still a limitation in the latest LLMs. The models are designed to generate human-like text based on the input they receive, but hallucinations (the generation of factually incorrect responses) can occur because the model is really only using probabilities to predict the next most likely word. One way this showed up in our early days of creating the math tutor was that the model was terrible at applying the distributive property. When given a problem like 4(2+x), it would say the answer to the next step was 8+x instead of 8+4x. In order to mitigate the risks of both getting these responses and having students trust every answer they received, we:

- used prompt engineering to improve math performance, including injecting the answer to the problem into the prompt and having the system check its math before responding to the student;
- developed a database of Khan Academy links so that when the model recommends content, it directs students toward helpful resources;
- displayed a message on every Khanmigo interaction screen to warn students that the model can be wrong and explain why;
- provided the means for users to report cases of incorrect responses and monitor those reports.

We believe these last two tactics are important for increasing AI literacy. If users understand the technology and its limits, they are more likely to monitor and check its answers, just as we hope learners do with answers from the internet. We are also hopeful that new, more advanced LLMs will continue to improve in response accuracy overall and specifically for math. We experienced an improvement from GPT-3.5 to GPT-4.0 in building Khanmigo, so we are confident that it will continue to get better.

Another issue related to accuracy involves possible biases embedded in large datasets and human-made algorithms. In our current sociopolitical climate, there are disagreements on what the truth is in many areas, including the impact of human activity on climate change, issues of sex and gender, and questions of race and racism, to name just a few. As a tool created by humans that draws on large, potentially flawed or incomplete data sets, AI is unfortunately subject to all of the same biases and blind spots as we are. Given that we haven't yet solved these problems as a society, it is not surprising that AI experiences the same problems. Potentially harmful, inaccurate outputs are a reality we have to contend with.

Addressing bad behavior

Much of the early conversation around generative AI in education, at least as shown in headlines of major news outlets, centered on the potential of AI-enabled tools to promote cheating. Students can go to ChatGPT to get the answer to almost any question or to get a reasonably well-written essay on many topics. We addressed this concern by:

- designing prompts to ensure that Khanmigo serves as a Socratic tutor—answering a question by asking the student another one— rather than giving away the answer;
- making transcripts of all chats viewable to the student, teacher, and parent if the student is under eighteen;
- developing activities and tools that allow students to outline and workshop essays with Khanmigo so that they can show their work to their teacher or parents.

None of this eliminates the possibility of students using publicly available AI tools for cheating, but it does mean that if parents and schools want students to be able to use AI-powered tools for learning, there are education-focused offerings available.

Another type of bad behavior is using the AI to promote violence, hate, or other potentially harmful content. We use a moderation tool (provided by OpenAI) in which every message receives a score on seven potential dimensions of harm (such as violence, hate, sexual content, and self-harm). We set thresholds for those scores above which we block the response from the model and notify parents and teachers of the message.

Bonus Challenge: Balancing Data Privacy and Model Bias

While generating a set of ethical principles takes time and thought, the real challenge happens when our principles conflict with one another. This is the case with our values of data privacy and reducing bias in models.

AI systems depend on data for personalized learning recommendations and predictions. The models are rightly criticized for being trained on data that are not representative of the diversity of the student population. To reflect this diversity, models need to be trained on more diverse data sets. However, this is in direct conflict with our value of student data privacy. Right now at Khan Academy, we guarantee our users that their data will not be used by OpenAI to train that company's models. We want districts to know that we respect the privacy of their data, and districts tell us that this is important to them. However, this means that the underlying models are not improved with data from our diverse groups of students and teachers.

OPPORTUNITIES FOR RETHINKING AI IN EDUCATION

Explore the Potential of AI

Everyone is in the early days of understanding and using generative AI tools. Even we, who had a few extra months to learn, are still discovering new uses for it. The current rate of development of AI technology means that school leaders will be in the unenviable position of making judgments about what to adopt based on limited information about AI and, likely, hundreds of pitches from vendors about what their tools can do.

We urge early adopters of AI systems to commit to an evaluation of those systems. Be clear about what the goals are for implementing an AI-powered system and how progress toward those goals will be monitored. In education, we have a system of end-of-year summative assessments that can be harnessed for this purpose. If we combine these assessments with the data the AI tutor gathers about use and interactions, we can learn what kinds of uses are having what kinds of impact.

Augment Human Intelligence with Artificial Intelligence

The rethinking of AI in education should not result in every student sitting alone, with headphones on, working independently all day. Instead, we can imagine a collaborative relationship between educators and AI. We should be thinking about how AI can help augment what human beings can do and help us lean into the skills that make us human. For example, in one school, administrators helped teachers brainstorm how best to engage students using Khanmigo. In another, teachers worked with their vice principal to use Khanmigo for differentiation of small-group instruction, augmenting what teachers already do in the classroom. This is the type of AI-human partnership that we should be striving toward.

Human beings are uniquely able to build meaningful relationships that motivate and sustain us. We know that peer-to-peer relationships are important for learning and that structured, collaborative learning experiences show improved learning outcomes. Adult–student relationships are important, too. Research tells us that students who have strong, positive relationships with adults in school are more likely to graduate.[20] But teachers need time to build these relationships with students and engage with them in deeper ways than simply asking them if their homework is done.

Even with improved memory and more robust student profiles, technology does not know the whole student (nor do we want it to). AI systems don't know that Ashley had a fight with her best friend at lunch or that Jordan is nervous about measuring up to his math-whiz twin sister. Of course, human beings have their own biases and habits of thinking, as well as limitations on how much they can do, see, and hold in their working memories. Nonetheless, human beings are uniquely able to transfer their understanding of the whole student to their educational plans.

THE FIRST YEAR

Khanmigo launched in March of 2023 to independent users and teachers, as well as to students in two districts and at the Khan Lab School. These districts were part of our Khan Academy Districts program, and large proportions of their students already used Khan Academy at least eighteen hours per year. In the fall of 2023, we extended Khanmigo district availability, and we have continued observing classrooms and interviewing students and teachers who are using it.

Our first observation is that many districts are eager to try it out in relatively small pilots, usually a couple hundred students in one or two content areas. Our second observation is that districts that were already using Khan Academy are having better experiences with Khanmigo. In part, this is because Khanmigo works best when it uses Khan Academy's content library as a reference. Also, Khanmigo is particularly good at helping students with independent practice, which many schools that already used Khan Academy had previously built into their schedules. Meanwhile, schools that are not familiar with the platform are learning both the platform and the AI interaction. In addition, some do not have dedicated independent practice time or do not utilize technology for that practice.

Our third observation is that teachers and students needed more time to learn how to interact with AI than we expected. First, they need to learn when Khanmigo might be helpful. Second, people who are just learning to use the tools often ask the AI to do something and, if they don't get the response they were looking for, give up and conclude that the AI can't do it, despite the fact that a few more interactions clarifying the request would often produce better results. For students, we are seeing that tutoring interactions are not as deep as we had hoped. We see a portion of students who just keep replying "I don't know" in response to questions. We are looking at ways to address the question of when to activate Khanmigo by having the AI tutor make the first interaction based on actions of the teacher or student (for example, the AI would step in after the student gets a question wrong). We are also exploring ways to teach students and teachers patterns of interactions and encouraging speech-to-text so students can talk instead of type to the tutor. Each of these addresses different hypotheses about barriers to effective use of learning tools.

CONCLUSION

When we were first approached by OpenAI to test GPT-4, we weren't sure of the capabilities of the model or of the most valuable use cases for education. We went through moments of excitement, disappointment, frustration, and optimism.

Now, more than a year after launching Khanmigo, we're seeing the benefits and the challenges through the eyes of our users. Students have shared that they feel motivated and empowered when they can work through a problem with Khanmigo. Teachers have been amazed by the amount of time our lesson planning activities save them and by the quality of output. And administrators see AI's potential to make learning relevant and personal—augmenting what teachers do best.

However, there are still challenges. Students want Khanmigo to remember their interests, to feel more like a tutor and less like a robot. They (understandably) get frustrated when Khanmigo makes mistakes. Some teachers have felt overwhelmed by learning a new tool and struggle to keep up with new releases. And administrators have dived into working with teachers on how to best use Khanmigo to personalize education.

We believe that generative AI can disrupt education, but we are fully aware of all the other technologies that have not made meaningful improvements in learning outcomes. Generative AI exists within a broader system of students, teachers, administrators, and parents, each of whom has different motivations and incentives. Any changes driven by generative AI are more likely to occur slowly and incrementally through our existing education structures. We do not predict a sudden shift away from students in physical classrooms with human teachers progressing through learning targets. In the short term, we expect students, teachers, administrators, and parents to continue dipping their toes into AI tools and using them to augment the learning experience in classrooms.

In the longer term, as we build awareness of the benefits of AI in education and increase AI literacy throughout the education system, we are more optimistic about the potential of generative AI. Teachers will be less burdened with administrative tasks and be able to focus more time on students. Students will be able to engage in more independent practice with the supports they need, and they will experience new kinds of interactions with digital tools that spark their curiosity and increase engagement in the activities we know accelerate learning. In such a world, generative AI could be the technology that finally moves the needle on learning outcomes.

2

Mastery Learning

Scott Ellis

It had been three weeks since a New York elementary school had started implementing my mastery learning software platform, and I was excited to get an update from the assistant principal in charge of teaching and learning. After she picked up the phone and we exchanged greetings, I asked her how it was going.

"Your system is causing hysteria in our school," she said. I was horrified, but she quickly reassured me. "Your system is great. It's just that we thought the students knew all these things . . . but they don't."

As we continued talking, we diagnosed the root causes of the challenges of implementation and discussed how mastery learning drastically changes so many fundamental aspects of teaching and learning. This brief conversation illustrated three themes that continue to shape the implementation of mastery learning in America's schools and districts: it has the potential to transform education, successful implementation requires educators to take several specific steps and support others along the way, and it is still a journey of innovation.

THE POTENTIAL TO TRANSFORM EDUCATION

I have spent over ten years working on mastery learning (sometimes called competency-based learning or proficiency-based learning) because I believe it is *the* transformational education innovation of our time. It enables students to progress at their own pace as they master content by clearly defining and measuring learning proficiency. This is in stark contrast to traditional methods of learning progression, which are based on time spent on a subject rather than mastery of it. In the past, the lack of technological infrastructure, software tools, and instructional practices made mastery learning impossible to scale. But now, for the first time ever, we have what we need to make it happen. My goal is to catalyze and accelerate the implementation of high-quality mastery learning in schools and districts across the US so we can maximize learning for all students.

Mastery learning increases student learning by making several specific improvements to the instructional process. First, it uses teaching and learning time more efficiently. Traditional practices waste precious student and teacher time by teaching all students the same thing at the same time, even though some students already know the content (and are bored), while others are still confused about the previous topic. In mastery learning, students learn the content they are ready to learn, making the learning process more efficient and allowing teachers to use their time more effectively.

Second, mastery learning increases and harnesses student motivation. I recently saw this quote at a community college near my home: "If you refuse to learn, no one can help you. If you are determined to learn, no one can stop you." (So true, today more than ever!) In other words, nothing cultivates learning more than an interested and determined student. Mastery learning helps ensure that students are neither bored nor lost, and that they can learn content that is at the right level for them. Students can approach learning in ways that are more interesting to them, and they can clearly define and measure their learning progress. When students have greater choice in what they learn, how they learn, and how they demonstrate mastery of what they have learned, their motivation increases.

Third, mastery learning has the potential to use new tools and technology effectively. A decade ago, few districts had devices for all students, and few educators used online mastery dashboards to monitor learning progress. Now, educators and leaders across the country use a wide range of software platforms and tools as part of their daily teaching and learning practices, and they understand their power and potential. While we are still just beginning to harness the power of these tools, we know that they have enormous potential to enable mastery learning and maximize learning for students.

Finally, in traditional classrooms, we primarily measure *teaching*, and this drives the timing of the educational process. Teachers must keep up with district pacing guides and make it through the textbook by the end of the semester. In mastery learning, we do not measure teaching. We measure *learning*. We don't focus on *how much teachers have taught*—we focus on *how much students have learned*. Then we implement processes and tools to make this happen over and over for every student.

Mastery learning brings these specific improvements to life in the classroom and harnesses them to improve student learning. However, whether students receive the full potential benefit depends on effective implementation.

STEPS TO SUCCESSFUL IMPLEMENTATION AND SUPPORT

Mastery learning is more possible than ever before. But it is new, and that means we are all still figuring out how to bring it to life in the classroom at scale. Most educators and leaders did not experience mastery learning when they were growing up, and most parents didn't either. As educators implement this new approach, they will need to take several specific steps and support both the kids and the adults in adapting to the changes involved.

Agree on Definitions and Key Principles

Educators and leaders must have a shared understanding of what they are implementing and what they are trying to achieve. Everyone should be able to articulate that they want to implement mastery learning, which means enabling students to move forward in their learning as they master content rather than as they advance through traditional "seat time" requirements.

Educators also need to agree that mastery is binary: either the student is ready to move on to a new learning objective or they need to keep working on the current one. When a student does not succeed in demonstrating mastery of an objective, it can be helpful to the teacher to know if the student is close to mastery or still has a long way to go. This enables the teacher to determine the appropriate next step in learning. To meet this need, it can be helpful to include a level of "near mastered" in addition to "not mastered." But there should only be one level of "mastered" and nothing above it. Once a student has mastered a learning objective, they should move on to another one. Additionally, students should be free to work on multiple objectives in parallel or to stop working on an objective for a time and come back to it later. They should not be required to work only on the one objective they are currently focused on, but they should be required to come back to each objective until they have demonstrated mastery.

Furthermore, educators should understand that any learning beyond mastery of the learning objective should be counted as progress toward a different, more advanced objective. If teachers implicitly have a more advanced learning objective and want some students to achieve an "exceeds" level, they should instead make an explicit additional learning objective that clearly tracks this level of learning and achievement—and it should be made available to all students.

The overall goals are twofold: to enable students to learn as much as they can, and to ensure that all students learn. When educators use the "exceeds" level, it is often to justify teaching all students the same content at the same time and moving at a pace set by students who need more time. This approach may have been needed in the past, when educators had fewer tools to enable personalization of learning, and it does simplify classroom management. But in mastery learning, we should seek to maximize learning and give students credit for everything they learn. Students should not spend additional time on an objective they have already mastered when the learning time could instead enable the student to make more progress.

Develop and Implement the Elements of Mastery Learning

While educators can (and must!) customize their approach to fit their environment and meet the needs of their students, mastery learning requires specific elements. Leaders and teachers must:

- define specific, clear, and demonstrable learning objectives;
- determine what it means for a student to meet the mastery threshold for each learning objective;
- decide how students will demonstrate mastery, whether by taking a test, presenting their findings, talking with a teacher, completing a project, or something else;
- determine how teachers will assess mastery, including whether they will leverage automated grading;
- decide how to monitor and display student learning progress, usually by selecting or designing a dashboard system in which data can be consistently updated.

Learning objectives and mastery thresholds are the core of the mastery learning architecture. As a skeleton does for a body, learning objectives provide the structure that organizes the mastery learning process and holds it together.

I saw the power of clear learning objectives and mastery thresholds in a Mandarin Chinese immersion program at a public elementary school in the San Francisco Bay Area. The teacher had been using texts that had been roughly leveled, meaning that the content and complexity of the text roughly aligned with defined levels of student reading capabilities. But the levels were vague, and it was very difficult for teachers to directly align reading materials to them. Some students did well in reading comprehension, while others struggled.

The school implemented a new mastery learning system with a foundation of specific learning objectives that were dramatically more explicit and included very clear mastery thresholds. The system also included texts that had been intentionally designed to align directly with the learning objectives for each level. Students advanced to a new level by mastering each of the objectives associated with the level. Using this new, clearer structure, the teachers assessed the students again. In the former system, they had been teaching all students at level G. With the new system, some students struggled at this level, and they were moved back to levels F or E, which better aligned with their knowledge. This was not surprising, since the students had struggled at level G, and the mastery system enabled the teachers to accurately determine their level of capability.

But what about the students who did well at level G? Under the new system, the teachers could assess the students at higher levels. Some of them did well at level H, or even I. The students kept going until they reached a level where they struggled with the assessments, at which point the teachers knew their students had found their true levels. A few students kept going further and mastered levels J, M, and P—and some even reached level S! The teachers were amazed but also horrified: they had been teaching these students at level G like everyone else, which was a tragic waste of precious learning time. The teachers were delighted to be able to provide better instruction based on their updated insights about what their students knew. Specific learning objectives and mastery thresholds made this possible.

The types of mastery thresholds for learning objectives in different subject areas vary widely. For some areas of math or physics, it may make sense for students to demonstrate mastery by solving problems, and so a mastery threshold might include a required level of accuracy (e.g., four correct out of five) within a given time period (e.g., three minutes). For a behavior objective in social and emotional learning (such as "treat others' belongings with respect"), it may be appropriate to require a student to first articulate what they are supposed to do and then to actually do it multiple times or do it consistently over a period of time. In language courses, students will often need to write papers or deliver speeches, and educators must define the specific mastery thresholds for learning objectives in these areas: what do we want the student to know or be able to do? The same is true in subjects like wood or metal shop, where students will need to follow specific procedures and create products. Many objectives are cumulative and build on previous skills or knowledge learned by a student, and this provides a good way of ensuring students remember content over time.

In a mastery learning system, there is no such thing as failure. Students may just not have mastered an objective yet, and they may need multiple attempts to demonstrate mastery. This is fine. But educators must design a process in which students have time to make multiple attempts, and teachers have time to assess multiple attempts. Sometimes teachers simply need more time for grading (to read a rewritten essay, for example), but much of this work can happen as part of the typical feedback and corrections that already exist as part of the teaching and learning process.

Teachers must also be able to quickly visualize the data about student learning status and progress. Mastery dashboards provide this information by displaying the mastery status for each learning objective for each student at a point in time. While these systems are still being developed and distributed in the marketplace, educators can also create simple versions using spreadsheets. The key is to define the data accurately and enable them to be displayed quickly.

Align Resources with Learning Objectives

Once educators have implemented the elements described above, mastery learning becomes possible. Next, resources must be aligned with each learning objective to enable students to learn and practice. Learning, practicing, and demonstrating mastery are discrete steps of the learning process. Educators must ensure students have access to the correct, aligned resources.

Since existing standards were not usually written with mastery learning in mind, the learning and practice resources rarely align with mastery learning objectives. This means educators must retrofit the existing resources onto the new structure of objectives. I encourage leaders and educators to identify and leverage resources other schools have already developed and only create new resources as a last resort. Their time is the most precious resource in education, so they must avoid reinventing the wheel whenever possible.

I helped one elementary school implement a mastery-based Spanish program for a few hundred students. Their existing curriculum had learning and practice resources for nearly all the old standards, which were vague. They had levels of oral proficiency associated with characteristics like creativity (repeating memorized words versus creating original sentences), text type (words, sentences, or paragraphs), frequency (most of the time, nearly all the time, or consistently), and comprehensibility (able to be understood by a parent, a sympathetic listener, or nearly anyone). We created clear, specific, and demonstrable learning objectives to precisely capture these elements—for example, *answer three highly familiar, open questions about daily life with single, complete sentences.* While the new mastery learning objectives we created were very different, teachers found that they did not need to create many brand-new resources or look for existing ones elsewhere. They were able to meet most of their needs with their existing books and other curricular elements by significantly reorganizing them to align with the new learning objectives. This was feasible because of the clarity of the learning objectives, and once they did it, they could use the content year after year in their mastery learning program.

The lack of learning and practice resources aligned with mastery learning objectives has delayed the widespread implementation of mastery learning. Current implementers stand on one side of a wide chasm. They can see the other side and the exciting possibilities it offers, but no one has built a bridge from one side to the other. There is a future state where all the elements of the mastery learning architecture exist and the path to mastery learning at scale stretches out before us. But we are simply not there yet. Those implementing mastery learning today don't need to create everything from scratch, but often they must modify or realign existing resources to meet new needs.

Redefine the Role of the Teacher

Once educators and leaders have cultivated all the elements of the mastery learning architecture, they can focus on redefining what the teacher does in the classroom. Teachers have the most vital role in education. How can we enable them to use their time in a way that maximizes student learning?

In mastery learning schools, teachers should not be the ones reworking existing standards into learning objectives, creating new learning objectives and mastery thresholds, or creating learning and practice resources. Once mastery learning has become well established, the learning objectives will already exist, and teachers will no longer have to translate existing standards into learning objectives. But we are not there yet. So for now, this is something teachers may need to do. Overall, educators should minimize time they spend on tasks like these and instead leverage the work of others. If it needs to be done, it should only be done once.

Indeed, teachers have better information about their students—and themselves—than anyone else in the system. They know their students as learners: who they are, what they like, what motivates them, and how they learn. They know themselves as educators: who they are, why they are teachers, what their strengths are, and how they like to work. With mastery dashboards, they also have accurate, real-time data about what their students know.

In mastery learning, teachers should continuously collect this precious information. They should aspire to know their students as well as possible so they can motivate and support their learning. They should reflect on their own strengths and interests as educators and constantly improve their practice. And they must analyze learning data consistently and use it to guide planning and instruction.

To achieve this goal, teachers should:

- constantly update student learning status on mastery dashboards;
- use data from these dashboards on an ongoing basis to monitor progress;
- develop and implement strategies for teaching and learning based on these data;
- use technology effectively to enable students to learn at different paces and in different ways—individually, in small groups, and in large groups;
- use student and teacher time flexibly to best meet the needs of all students;
- require that all students learn; this may mean allocating teacher time very differently than in traditional classrooms (such as by spending very different amounts of time with different students or groups of students);
- repeat the process, update the data, and adapt based on what works for students.

Teachers have unique information and expertise. They also have critical work to do and very little time to do it. To make the profession appealing and sustainable, we also need teachers to have balanced, sane lives. We must ensure that their precious time is used as effectively and efficiently as possible, all with the goal of maximizing student learning.

Establish Appropriate Levels and Types of Student Choice

Students should have a choice about how they demonstrate mastery, meaning that educators should provide multiple approaches that are equally valid. Students may also have a choice about how they learn a skill. Providing choice in these two aspects of mastery learning can engage learners in different ways and increase their ownership and therefore their motivation. But students should not get unfettered choice about what they learn and at what pace.

I often hear people say they want students to learn at their own pace. But what happens if the student's pace is a bit too leisurely (as may be the case for struggling students)? I encourage the educators I work with to establish a negotiated pace, meaning that the teacher and the student agree together on the desired pace of learning. In a negotiated pace, students have choice, but it is carefully defined and managed.

Student choice about what to learn is also important but limited. For example, as a parent, taxpayer, and community member, I believe my school district should be accountable for ensuring that every graduate can multiply a one-digit number by a two-digit number. On the other hand, I do not believe every student should be required to master calculus. This is something students should be able to choose.

Another reasonable limitation on student choice is defining the threshold for mastery. If a student decides they want to master calculus, they may have choices about how they learn and how they demonstrate mastery, but they do not get to define what mastery means. This should be defined by education experts.

Student choice is a critical aspect of mastery learning and offers opportunities to cultivate and harness learner motivation. But choice is a nuanced topic, and educators should clearly define where they are offering students choice, where they are not, and why.

IMPLEMENTATION CHALLENGES ALONG THE JOURNEY OF INNOVATION

Although researchers and educators have talked about mastery learning for many years, few schools have implemented it at scale. This approach is still new, and it transforms fundamental aspects of the teaching and learning process. Logistical obstacles, the challenges of managing change, and the daily realities of running schools can all impede progress. We can overcome these obstacles, but doing so demands patience, determination, and creativity. The path to success will not be a straight line; it will be a meandering journey of trial and error, continuous improvement, and collaboration.

Logistical Obstacles

The US K–12 education system is not mastery-based and therefore does not use mastery grading. Instead, the system is based on traditional seat-time requirements, A through F grading, and assessments based on grade-level standards instead of clear, specific, demonstrable learning objectives. These traditional measures are embedded in college and university admissions processes and, since K–12 stakeholders value postsecondary admissions, they ripple down through preschool. Although some colleges and high schools are starting to accept mastery transcripts, traditional grades are still the norm, and feeder schools hesitate to adopt mastery learning.

Several years ago I worked with the president of a small university in Maine who said her institution sought applicants from mastery learning high schools because she "didn't want to spend the first three semesters teaching new students to be in charge of their own learning." However, few of her colleagues share this refreshing perspective. One of my K–8 client schools near Oakland chose not to continue a very successful implementation because they were concerned their students would struggle to gain admission to high schools whose application processes required traditional report cards and grades. This is a tough barrier to overcome, though progress is coming.

When elite universities like Harvard and Stanford begin to give preference to students with mastery transcripts, the K–12 market will move. But until then, innovators will struggle to convince high schools (and the parents of their students) to adopt new approaches to teaching and learning. This will cascade down to middle and elementary schools as well. Some schools attempt to convert mastery-based grades to traditional grades, but standardized approaches have not yet been developed to do so. This remains a major issue.

State regulations that impose specific seat-time requirements on K–12 schools present another major logistical challenge. Seat-time requirements directly contradict the premises of mastery learning because they define success by how long a student works on a topic rather than whether they have learned it. In mastery learning, we care only about what a student knows, and time spent learning is irrelevant. These regulations affect ongoing learning as well as graduation requirements.

How schools assess learning also presents challenges. One elementary charter school in New York was very excited about my mastery learning math program and asked whether they should get rid of their existing district benchmark assessments and just use the mastery structure. My response: not yet—it is still too early. Instead, I advised my client to use mastery learning as the core instructional process while they continued with the existing assessments. They could not change whether a student was required to take an exam on a particular date, but since they had the data from the mastery learning system, they would know in advance how the student would likely perform, and they could use this information to target learning support for the student as effectively as possible.

Finally, the tools needed to track and assess student learning progress are not yet adequate. Educators still do not have simple mastery dashboards connected to learning systems to meet their needs. This means teachers often improvise their own dashboards, which is a tremendous draw on their time. While automated grading can save teachers significant time, it is not widely implemented or available, and many subjects do not lend themselves to such technology. But as these systems improve, they will save teachers time and improve student learning.

Early adopters of mastery learning must decide how to manage all of these elements—transcripts, seat-time requirements, assessments, and data systems—when trying to innovate within the current system. They may choose to run processes in parallel or seek waivers to enable innovation. Although many existing structures and regulations use time-based metrics and processes, it's still too soon for mastery learning educators to fully unplug them.

The Challenges of Managing Change

Principals, teachers, parents, and students all need help understanding how mastery learning changes the daily experience of education. Without support, their concerns and struggles will grow and could undermine implementation and buy-in.

Mastery learning can be extremely powerful and positive, but educators need to help everyone understand what is happening and why. For instance, as described at the beginning of this chapter, parents and teachers—and students—may feel extremely anxious when students do not demonstrate mastery of learning objectives that teachers think they already know. However, there are often real gaps in student learning that were previously hidden. I have often had teachers thank me for helping them uncover student learning gaps they couldn't find through traditional grading.

Students and parents also need to understand the implications of the fact that there is no failure in a mastery system. Students still must master the material—we are not lowering the bar for performance. However, we can accomplish this while reducing stress for students. I talked with a high school senior from Los Angeles who attended a mastery learning school. She said she particularly liked mastery learning because it eliminated the panic she and her classmates felt in traditional schooling. For example, she had a significant physics test that week. She was stressed and studying hard. But she said the old feeling of sheer panic she used to experience was gone. Why? Because she knew that if she did not do well, she could relearn the material, study, and take the test again. To be clear, she badly wanted to avoid this outcome—she needed to learn the material and be successful on the test, and she did not want to spend the time required to learn again and retest. But there was no panic: if she did poorly, the grade would not sit on her transcript (and college applications!) forever. This aspect of mastery learning should be clearly explained to students and parents. What matters is not getting it right the first time; what matters is the actual learning.

Mastery learning sometimes reveals unexpected but necessary changes in the basic steps of teaching and learning, like the importance of teachers taking time before starting new content to be sure students understand what they are learning and why it matters. This is a significant mindset shift. One middle school math teacher at a public school in Salt Lake City described the challenges faced by some of his best students in the traditional system once he implemented mastery learning. These students were "good at school" because they responded well to direction and did what they were told, but they really struggled with the choice and opportunities for self-direction offered by mastery learning. Students asked questions like, "What is my homework tonight?" or "How many points is this assignment worth?" and struggled to internalize the implications when the teacher replied, "We're doing mastery learning now. We don't think like that anymore." At one point, one of the students came up to him and said, "I would appreciate it if you would just tell me what to do." The same teacher also described students who could tell him what learning objective they were working on but couldn't articulate its meaning or significance. He decided to change his teaching practice to remedy this situation and said he should have been fully explaining the objectives all along.

Parents can also struggle to internalize the philosophy and implications of mastery learning. Sometimes the best solution is for parents to engage directly with the mastery learning data for their children. We can only explain so much, especially since so many aspects of the new approach differ from how parents learned themselves. One of my clients at a large international elementary school in Singapore told me how much mastery learning changed the parent-teacher conference experience and the nature of parent involvement in the education process. In the previous year, one of their students with engaged parents with high expectations was struggling. When the teacher described the student's performance at the parent-teacher conference, the parent bluntly said to the teacher, "Well, that must be because you are doing something wrong." The next year in their parent-teacher conference, the same teacher shared a mastery dashboard with the same parent and showed the specific learning objectives their child had not yet mastered. The parent reviewed the data, paused, turned to the student, and said, "Well, I guess now we know what to work on at home tonight." Students and parents need to be prepared for greater clarity about student learning than they have ever had, which means leaders and educators must invest significant additional time to help their community adjust to the new approach.

The Daily Realities of Running Schools

Running schools is hard. Sometimes challenges completely unrelated to mastery learning can delay or even end implementation. One of my K–8 client schools had hired a new principal over the summer, but then was informed one week before the start of the school year that she wasn't coming after all. They faced existential challenges, and so they decided to stop implementation. I fully supported their decision. While this is an extreme example of leadership instability, any leadership change can disrupt the process of implementing mastery learning—or any innovation in schools.

Today, many other issues are affecting and distracting educators (student safety; state legislation related to issues of equity, race, and gender; etc.). Schools are complicated institutions embedded in complex and evolving communities, and the concerns and dynamics of families, governments, and leaders impact the way schools operate every day. I have been in multiple meetings with school leaders that were abruptly ended because a shooting had occurred in a nearby school. When this happens, everything stops, because student safety supersedes everything. School board meetings around the country are regularly required to focus on topics unrelated to the daily mechanics of student learning. When this happens, it is very difficult for educators to prioritize innovation in pedagogy.

This is the reality of education in twenty-first-century America. Every organization has limits to the amount of change it can tolerate, and innovation is one of many types of change.

Even during times with lots of potential for change, the implementation challenges schools face can be overwhelming. When the pandemic hit in 2020, many colleagues reached out to me and said, "At last! Now is the time for mastery learning! Schools are looking for something like this to help navigate the pandemic." But this is not what happened. Schools faced immense new challenges executing basic online schooling, then grappled with transitioning between remote and in-person school, and finally resumed full in-person operations in a new world. They were just trying to survive. They did not have the organizational bandwidth to incorporate a transformational change in core teaching and learning. This reality will continue to limit innovation in education in the years ahead.

FINAL THOUGHTS

My work has focused on K–12 education, but over the past few years, I have also implemented these principles with adult learners. Mastery learning is especially applicable in the labor market, where a hiring manager seeks a candidate who is able to do a specific list of things. I have built mastery-based manager training programs for nonprofit CEOs and developed mastery-based role descriptions for disaster responders. The same principles that apply to adult learning also apply to K–12 education. Although mastery learning has transformational potential, it is also straightforward. This is how much of the real world works, whether we are talking about a hiring process, an individual learning to play guitar, or a family trip: we determine where we are, define where we want to go, figure out how to get there, and then make progress toward our goal step by step. We should teach students in this way to prepare them to take ownership of their own performance and learning throughout their lives.

Implementing mastery learning remains a journey of innovation. It has tremendous potential to transform teaching and learning, but it is still new and requires persistence, clear communication, and effective management of change. I hope new leaders, educators, parents, and students will join me in this effort and keep these final thoughts in mind along the way:

- *Focus on clear learning objectives and mastery thresholds.* These are the core elements of the entire mastery learning architecture.
- *Measure learning, not teaching.* Gather accurate real-time data about student learning, update it continuously, and use it to drive the entire teaching and learning process.
- *Remember: This is innovation!* Things may not work the first time, and that's okay. Start small, learn, and improve. Gradually we can build the future of learning—together.

3

Rethinking Personalization

A SYSTEM FEATURE FOR THE FUTURE OF SCHOOLING

Beth Rabbitt

I'd wager most readers can identify moments when they needed more individual flexibility and support in their own lives. Most likely, some of these moments occurred in school. As a student with learning differences who moved schools a lot, I know this firsthand. Having to repeatedly plug into new school communities, sometimes midyear and across state lines, meant I developed significant gaps in knowledge and relationships. The gaps multiplied with every year and transition. By my seventh school and twelfth grade, I felt lost. The system couldn't meet my needs.[1] I nearly didn't make it out of high school, educationally or generally. (Ultimately, and thankfully, I did. My school didn't help.)

I offer my story for two reasons. The first is that it helps explain why I've spent the better part of two decades supporting innovation and improvement in schools, and I now lead The Learning Accelerator (TLA). TLA is a nonprofit intermediary that is building an education field where practitioners, leaders, and policymakers can learn faster and change systems together to ensure every student gets what they need to fulfill their unique potential.

The second reason is to make concrete how it feels to be a student who "fails to fit" the system, what the consequences of that can be, and why we shouldn't tolerate it. I'm infuriated that we can tell a version of my story for so many learners, the vast majority of whom are less privileged than I am and was. We routinely fail kids incrementally and seismically, leaving extraordinary amounts of human talent, genius, and joy on the table.

That's where personalization comes in. Personalization is the ability to reliably and meaningfully meet individual needs within the context of a system. When it's done right, it's an effective way to manage the tension between the dual aims of efficiency for many (increasing access and quality of goods) and effectiveness for each (offering customization to specific individuals and communities). Accelerated by technological innovation, personalization has become a critical feature of high performing systems across numerous industries from health care to investment banking. Across several domains, efforts abound to offer greater personal support and choice within systems and at scale.

Perhaps nowhere is this work more complex, and necessary, than in education, where we are challenged to consistently deliver quality and equity at scale to a diverse group of individuals. As humans develop and change, we are challenged to do it again and again.

Given this, it seems obvious that personalization should be a core feature of our K–12 public education systems. But it isn't. Roughly a century into the establishment of compulsory, common schooling, we face persistent, overall low performance. We see pernicious, demographically predictable gaps in achievement and opportunity at the group level, with significant microlevel variation. Nearly two-thirds of students leave high school disengaged in their learning, and the percentage of school-age children enrolled in public schools—a powerful metric of confidence—is on the decline.[2]

These statistics point to a systemic failure to address unique learner needs. Even in instances where we have invested in increased support for individuals, such as recent massive investments in high-dosage tutoring and mentorship programs, the vast majority of efforts to personalize happen around the margins of the student experience.

We can do better, and kids deserve it.

Calls for better understanding our students and tailoring more flexible approaches based on that knowledge have arisen from nearly every corner of the education sector. I propose that we already know a lot about how to accomplish this goal. I also want to offer a set of lessons derived from TLA's last decade of work to help guide us forward:

- Personalization is a feature of a system, not a distinct or competing model.
- We know a lot about the practices that increase personalization.
- Personalization requires systematic capacity building with a long-term view.
- Adhering to core principles can help create more durable and equitable personalization for learners in the future.

PERSONALIZATION AS A FEATURE, NOT A MODEL

Personalization is an attribute that systems can design for, not a distinct model for teaching and learning in and of itself. Fundamentally, it is the ability to meet individual needs reliably and meaningfully within the context of system delivery. There are three key attributes of personalization to keep in mind as you read the rest of this chapter.

Personalization is a process that happens across sectors and domains of human experience. It involves different strategies in different domains, from learning to read to training for a marathon, and requires an understanding of which strategies work best for whom. Personalization can involve and be designed within different modalities—analog and digital—as well as individually and for groups. And personalization can take place to different degrees.

Personalization is not an outcome, nor is it inherently good or bad. Our sector often layers qualitative modifiers on definitions, turning clear definitions into subjective hopes ("Personalized learning empowers every child with confidence!"). This makes it impossible to talk about outcomes. The value of personalization is determined by how well it *reliably and meaningfully* meets the individual needs of a learner while balancing costs and benefits considered alongside other group and individual goals. It can also happen at different depths, with experiences being more or less personalized.

Personalization as a singular model does not scale. How we personalize varies wildly because contexts and individual needs vary wildly. Bundling together personalization strategies as a model and trying to replicate them with strict fidelity across contexts doesn't work. It just grafts the challenge of applying a one-size-fits-all approach to learning onto a one-size-fits-all approach to personalizing all schools or communities. For this reason, there isn't one "right" scalable model. This doesn't mean models that maximize personalization aren't useful; rather, we have no evidence they can scale *as models.* It is much more useful to articulate specific teaching and learning problems in a particular context (lack of engagement, challenges in differentiating for specific student subgroups, etc.) and explain to educators how they can use personalization strategies to try to solve them.

Understanding what personalization is—and what it is not—makes it possible to define specific practices that can be understood, adopted, and adapted within and across local contexts. We can offer frameworks that help educators understand and select strategies for personalization based on their needs and resources. We can build capacity for personalization that is both scalable and sustainable.

PRACTICES THAT INCREASE PERSONALIZATION

In mid-2015, interest in launching and scaling personalized learning models began increasing. This cycle was fueled by several high-profile publications—including *The End of Average* by Todd Rose and *Disrupting Class* by Clayton Christensen, Curtis Johnson, and one of this volume's editors, Michael Horn—as well as by emerging charter exemplars supported by new technology platforms like Summit Learning and several high-profile funder initiatives, such as the Gates Foundation's Next Generation Systems Initiative, which aimed to scale personalized learning approaches in a set of major districts.

Despite this energy, personalization remained theoretical. Competing frameworks and definitions abounded, but actionable guidance and concrete examples of schools and districts executing more personalized approaches to learning sustainably and at any level of scale were absent.

TLA launched a large research project to fill this gap and identify practices that schools were using to personalize education. We reviewed over a hundred schools that were implementing personalized strategies, visiting a third of them to identify the specific techniques they were using and to understand and document their work. Our goal was to make these strategies available to others. We created an open and growing database of personalized learning practices and a series of case studies to show how different schools were bundling them into distinct models.[3]

We found that strong systems that emphasize personalization choose different approaches, but each strives to meet four critical needs of learners: personal relevance and targeted support, active engagement, social connection, and growth orientation. We also codified four specific practices associated with these approaches and learner needs.

Personal Relevance and Targeted Support

Students enter age-based classrooms with different types of experiences, motivations, cultural foundations, and levels of knowledge and skill. They pay the most attention to things that are salient and interesting to them and to information that is placed within their existing domain of knowledge and is close to their skill level. Effective personalization identifies and responds to these differences.

Educators can ensure each student has experiences aligned to achieve learning goals and tailored to their unique needs, strengths, interests, and identities. Common strategies to do this include:

- combining rigorous, grade-level learning with individual and small-group instruction;
- using differentiated pathways and materials;
- engaging in culturally relevant teaching.

Active Engagement

Learning is an active experience that requires students to attend to, engage with, and cognitively process new materials. To do this, they must connect new information with existing knowledge, elaborate on and generalize ideas to increase understanding, and use new skills in different contexts.

Educators can ensure that activities are planned and executed in ways that encourage deep interaction with content, build individual motivation and ownership, and support the transfer of new knowledge and skills to different applications. Common strategies include:

- choice and self-directed learning;
- authentic inquiry and application of ideas to projects and tasks;
- opportunities for explicitly activating and reflecting on prior knowledge and mastery.

Social Connection

Human brains are wired for social connection, action, and work. Learning deepens when students have opportunities to share their thinking and processing with others. Moreover, students are more likely to attend to higher-order thinking and learning when they experience positive relationships and attachments. This enables them to feel safe, which further increases their engagement and resiliency.

In personalized classrooms, educators can encourage and enable students to make meaningful, supportive connections with teachers, experts, peers, and the content they're learning. Common strategies include:

- offering peer learning and collaboration;
- establishing and explicitly reinforcing relationships and trust;
- building family and community engagement and connection in learning.

Growth Orientation

Developing a growth mindset, the ability to self-direct learning, and the ability to reflect on one's own thinking are all positively associated with long-term academic outcomes. Students need to understand where they are in their learning as well as have opportunities to apply strategies that increase understanding and reinforce learning over time. This works especially well when schools measure success in terms of mastery rather than the time spent on a task or completion.

Personalized learning experiences build intentionally toward mastery. With mastery, students can develop a clear understanding of where they are and where they are going, receive feedback from teachers, demonstrate competency, and plan next steps. Common strategies include:

- setting goals and planning;
- practicing deliberately for sustained periods;
- responding to actionable feedback for improvement;
- monitoring and reporting progress.

SYSTEMATIC CAPACITY BUILDING WITH A LONG-TERM VIEW

Personalized practices exist in many classrooms, but they scale with depth, breadth, and durability when they become a core feature within a system. My team and I have spent time in hundreds of schools and thousands of classrooms observing educators working to make this a reality. We've reviewed frameworks, definitions, blogs, research reports, and briefs that lay out the theory and evidence. We've watched systems scale personalized approaches, and we've also watched them lose steam and fail. I've seen that the most sustained, deep personalization happens in systems that have:

- visions that are grounded in problems that personalization can help solve;
- embedded, balanced strategies that avoid or mitigate known problems;
- conditions that support coherence and sustainability.

Visions and Objectives

When we talk about implementations focused on personalization, the focus is often on the nuts and bolts of *what* (the strategy or solution) and *how* (the process). The strongest implementations we at TLA have identified tend to start instead with a very clear *why*. The *why*s vary and offer different on-ramps to change. Here are three examples:

Redesigning long-term to enact a new strategic vision

In California's Lindsay Unified School District, leader Tom Rooney and his team have grounded their long-term *why* in the district's strategic plan, a community-created vision that was adopted in 2007 and has driven their work for over fifteen years. The vision emerged from data that showed significant failures in meeting the needs of their student body, which was made up largely of students coming from Central Valley farming communities. With roughly one-quarter of students meeting proficiency standards in reading and math, leaders saw students struggling after graduating from high school, with one article reporting that the class valedictorians who enrolled in the University of California system typically became mired in remedial courses.[4] After reviewing these data, the community recognized the need to do something different, so it instigated a community redesign and a complete shift toward performance-based learning. Leaders dismantled systems, built new technologies, and adopted new language for talking about the work. (As a partner to the district, we learned to use the terms *learner* and *facilitator* instead of *student* and *teacher*.)

Tackling a persistent equity challenge

At Leadership Public Schools, a high school charter organization, the former leaders Louise Bay Waters and Michael Fauteux grounded their *why* in a pernicious challenge for math learning. Students were entering ninth grade at wildly different mastery levels. Leadership Public Schools needed to ensure that learners at least mastered algebra in order to enable every student to access college. They designed and rolled out a new academic numeracy program called Navigate Math, a mastery-based course that students took alongside their grade-level group course. By blending a mix of small-group and individual instruction and using open educational resources, dedicated teachers closed learning gaps and accelerated learning:

students gained an average of 2.8 math grade levels per year on the Northwest Evaluation Association MAP assessment.

Responding to urgent, novel conditions

In Ector County Independent School District, a rural district in Texas's Permian Basin, superintendent Scott Muri had just wrapped up sharing a new strategic plan when the pandemic hit. The plan centered on preparing learners for the future of work, and it articulated a series of foundational technological, budgeting, and operational goals that Muri thought would take years to implement. However, by tapping into the urgent need to serve students well through closures and reopening (their *why*), Muri was able to accelerate his five-year plan and reorganize it into one year by making huge investments in infrastructure, like universal broadband, and new personalization tactics, such as virtual tutoring and the use of New Classrooms, a personalized math program founded by Joel Rose (a fellow contributor to this volume).

Looking across these examples, it's clear that there isn't a single *why* or pathway to making personalization a core feature, but there are common principles for setting and maintaining efforts:

- *Learner-centered orientation.* Successful visions and plans don't confuse the act of learning with strategies like "digital" or "competency-based." While those strategies can help further the goals of education, they are secondary to the student experience.
- *Clear purpose.* Personalization efforts are grounded in real, relevant, visible equity needs felt by the community.
- *Connection.* A developed vision for learning requires community buy-in and engagement.
- *Coherence.* Visions and plans communicate the need to tackle both practices at the core of learning and surrounding conditions like policy.
- *Comprehensiveness.* Visions recognize and articulate a plan to remove the structural "load-bearing walls" (time, staffing, etc.) and free up resources for deeper, long-term change.[5]

Embedded, Balanced Strategies

I've written already about the aims of personalization and how educators implement them in different configurations. Here are a few that are worth noting.

First, educators must acknowledge and balance seemingly competing priorities. Because we prefer stories with heroes and villains, we often pit different theories of change against one another. This is also true for efforts to personalize: it's personalized *or* group-based, which we refer to with norm-laden language like *modernized* or *antiquated* and *traditional* or *progressive*. We can pit personalization against standardization as well, but reality is much more complicated because education must balance demands arising from both collective and individual needs.

Consider support for learners who are multilingual. Using technology to offer content in a native language can support students learning English because it allows them to access learning that would otherwise be inaccessible. However, learning from virtual content alone can reduce opportunities for peer-to-peer learning and dialogue. The decision to use a personalization strategy has trade-offs, and we must be vigilant to ensure we're not falling into equity traps.

Unchecked personalization can prioritize individual learning at the cost of important social and collective experiences that could be more beneficial. Dan Meyer, director of research at Amplify and a strong critic of personalized learning, points out that many recent initiatives failed to consider how skilled educators can "put learner variability to good use" in group-based learning activities that increase opportunities for student inquiry, understanding, and dialogue.[6] We've seen this same dynamic in attempts to personalize health care. The medical field has taken huge strides toward personalized care via targeted therapies, genomic testing, and precision medicine. However, those efforts have had to be balanced with population-based measures like vaccination to prevent known diseases from wreaking havoc.

Another pitfall is failing to recognize that students need to have good relationships, strong attachments, and consistent routines to maximize learning. Early personalized school models encouraged students to work with teams of adults based on specific learning tasks and needs. Many of these designers backtracked once they realized how this affected their youngest learners. Juggling so many adult relationships and unpredictable schedules undermined students' need for secure relationships, trust, and predictability. It also exacerbated inequities, with the largest negative impacts felt by kids who had experienced trauma or were navigating instability at home.

Educators need to seek balance in aims and approaches. Treating personalization as one strategy among many supports stronger student outcomes.

Conditions That Support Coherence and Sustainability

Personalization can't be successful if it's at odds with the underlying system. In fact, the strongest implementations we've seen invest heavily in building the system—the supports, structures, and processes—that can support scale and consistency of personalized practice across classrooms and schools.[7]

Many systems must be put in place, but I want to focus here on two of them.

Infrastructure

One of the oddest aspects of the debates around personalization is that they often end up in the land of false dichotomies. Instructional infrastructure initiatives such as Common Core State Standards and, more recently, the high-quality instructional materials movement are routinely pitted against strategies for personalization.

It's better to think of infrastructure and personalization in terms of relationship polarity: they both need each other in the same way breathing in requires breathing out. You can't personalize anything with consistency and rigor if you're not building on a strong, coherent base. You need assessments, data, and related standards or competencies to do any meaningful targeted instruction. Similarly, personalization—including through tutoring, opportunities for individual practice, and the modification of materials—can help students achieve proficiency in common standards because it can help make learning more cognitively relevant. Strong implementation teams recognize this and build both.

Resource reallocation

Personalization can become unsustainable when leaders fail to critically examine how resources—time, people, technology, and space—can be unlocked from traditional structures. Layering personalization on top of already inefficient systems creates challenges from the get-go.

Aside from initial investments in things like training, technology, and building remodeling, we often see that once resources are reallocated schools can implement more radical personalized models on traditional budgets. In our review of implementations, nearly every organization has scrutinized existing usage and decided to make changes that give more flexibility and energy back to teachers and students. Whether through multiteacher staffing structures, blended learning approaches, multiage classrooms, flexible physical campuses, or otherwise, leaders move resources to enable change.

CORE PRINCIPLES FOR DURABLE, EQUITABLE PERSONALIZATION

We've learned a lot about what personalization can look like in systems that organize around it. But what about the broader sector of individuals and organizations supporting, informing, and advocating for this work? What factors and ideas might we hold at the forefront of debates, policy, and design?

Make Learners the Center of Gravity

The mental models we use to identify challenges, and the language we use to describe these challenges, are powerful. However, language and thinking that puts adults at the center of systems of organizing fail to get us to the level of specificity we need to improve learning for individual students.

At TLA, we try very hard to build frameworks that center on the needs and experiences of individual learners. For example, consider the term *learning loss*. Learning loss describes a system-level expectation of learning growth across a heterogeneous group of students. From a practical perspective, it's relatively useless. Which students lost what? Why and how? Did they have "it" to begin with? If we respond to system learning loss, we prioritize batch solutions designed to accelerate against an average.

It is much more beneficial to think about student-level "unfinished learning." This perspective asks us what concepts and skills each student had an opportunity to be exposed to, whether they mastered them, and, if not, how to support their progress toward mastery. Personalized and targeted strategies can be built from there.

Learn and Reflect on the Lessons of the Past

Efforts to personalize K–12 learning here in the US go back hundreds of years.[8] I nearly failed the one history class I took in college (a fact that causes my historian spouse much glee), but even I know that we ignore the origins of current practice and policy at our peril.

Across the historical arc of US public education, we've cycled through various efforts to enact reforms, some aimed at greater personalization and others at increasing system-level capacity and standardization.

Take, for example, age-based cohorts and A to F grading. They are frequent fodder for the scorn of innovation advocates, who proclaim them the result of intentional, nefarious efforts to batch-process kids to build an industrial workforce. I will not argue that forces of elitism, racism, and capitalism were not at play. However, I will say that the more nuanced story offers insight into the challenges of systems change and improvement we face today.

Age-based cohorts and A to F grading were adopted when reformers sought to move away from systems that emphasized subject-based individualization and ranking systems that organized learners into level-based cohorts. These approaches were executed in small-group formats with tutors—working under a master teacher—to address specific mastery progressions. They also presented a few problems:

- These individualized, coordinated approaches proved difficult to scale in increasingly large, urban environments. The complexity of student grouping and movement made management impossible.

- The assessment and communication of mastery was often based on subjective standards of master teachers and emphasized within-class standing.
- These approaches to ranking inflicted social stigma on learners who were further behind and made it difficult for learners to move between schools and districts because of the relative subjectivity of grading.

Reformers saw a model that grouped by age and offered a more standardized, objective form of grading system (A to F) as a way to solve these challenges.[9]

It's startling to note that the challenges reformers tackled a hundred years ago have similar characteristics to the solutions—including high-dosage tutoring, personalized learning pathways, and multiclassroom lead teachers—being discussed today. I don't mean to imply they are doomed or wrongheaded; many are promising, backed by evidence, and easier to implement at scale thanks to modern technologies.

However, as we now consider their implementation as part of broader systems, producing different results will require attention to the connections and failures of the past.

Focus on Evolving Social Systems, Not Rolling Out Solutions

In the fall of 2019, TLA embarked on a project to understand the strategies and conditions for longer-term change in school systems that had scaled and sustained personalized models. In a conversation with Scott Frauenheim, the then-CEO of Distinctive Schools, I asked how CICS West Belden's pilot—done in partnership with LEAP Innovations, which Scott now leads—had scaled across grades and other campuses. "Given how much success we'd had, and how much enthusiasm there was in other grades, I thought taking the tools the pilot team had developed to additional teams would be easy," he reflected. "But it wasn't the tools the new teams needed: it was a version of the design process itself. We realized they needed to go through their own learning, aligned to a 'why,' to be able to use the tools now available in our system."

We often forget that we are in the business of human development and that schools and districts are social systems—not mechanistic ones—created and transformed by the people within them.[10] We must attend to the development and learning of not just our students but also our adults.

This is inconvenient. We'd love to be able to simply design a new solution, train on it, and watch it take root. But we must remember to build community capacity into our planning and management of change.

DON'T LET THE PIGEON DRIVE THE BUS!

Don't Let the Pigeon Drive the Bus! is a celebrated children's book by Mo Willems. It features a pigeon who is dying to drive a bus while its driver is taking a break. Readers, typically preschoolers, are encouraged to just say "No!" through the pigeon's escalating requests and tantrums.

I haven't focused much on technology in this piece in part because, while it's an essential tool, it is not a wholesale solution. But I'd be remiss to ignore it. Technology access and advancement will be a critical force for making personalization more feasible, for more kids, with improved quality and sustainability over time. However, with due respect to colleagues working in education technology and funding, we let the pigeon drive the bus when we allow technology-based theories of change to dominate.

One pattern of pigeon driving is what I call the "platform hype cycle." Learning platforms are great, and we must invest in ones that align with more personalized approaches. However, a pattern has emerged:

- *Hope.* An innovative school creates a customized platform to support its model. The success garners attention and interest in replication.
- *Hype.* Funders are drawn to the platform and invest in the tech by creating a platform provider to help the model scale. The platform is adopted in more schools.
- *Implementation challenges.* Schools need implementation support to replicate the nontech, systemic conditions necessary for quality. Providers invest in technical assistance capacity to address challenges of scale and consistency. This work is substantively different from simple technology investment, requiring more time and hands-on support.
- *Capacity strain.* Given expanding demand for technical assistance, providers hire the experts who led the work at the original sites, weakening the implementation.

- *Competing sustainability needs.* The complexity and economics of managing a platform versus a deep technical assistance organization becomes untenable. The platform remains viable as support for a smaller subset of schools, but development resources become scarce. Initiative leaders decide to separate the technology entity from the technical assistance entity, given competing needs and opportunities to pursue different forms of investment (typically, for-profit capital versus philanthropic support).
- *Abandonment.* The technology is sold to or adopted by an organization with resources. To make the economics work, this organization needs to make the product more marketable to a broader set of schools, with less personalization and freer operating rules. Similarly, the technical assistance provider moves to more general model support and change management to tap into a broader range of clients and models.

This is a generalization, but I can apply this story to many platform-focused initiatives, ranging from well-known examples like Alt School and Summit Learning to lesser-known examples like Highlight, Spark, and Gooru. We don't have a compelling case that platform-centric theories drive the change we want.

DELIVERING PERSONALIZATION AT SCALE

I was up early working on this chapter when my youngest daughter emerged from her bedroom, plopped down next to me, and asked me what I was doing. I shared I was writing about how we could make schools work better for kids. She exclaimed, "Mom, I have the best ideas on this!" and went on to detail a vision for a school without grade levels, where "All the kids would get to learn in the spaces they wanted to, work on the things they most needed help with, and could go to lunch or use the bathroom whenever they wanted. But only if they were getting their work done."

My daughter's vision ballooned into a multiday project with a hand-drawn school diagram, speeches, and the bending of adult ears. Holding up her drawing to anyone who would listen, she began the same way every time: "Look at this. What do you notice?" Several days into her quest, I mentioned that I work with many schools that look a lot like what she's described. "You do? Why haven't you fixed this yet?" she demanded.

Why haven't we? Beyond our habit of ignoring history and the complexity of this work, the education sector lacks the structures and practices to learn. We struggle to track progress, tap into existing knowledge, and leverage strategies from other sectors and professions. Our efforts are often siloed and competitive. Our economic and resource engines encourage proprietary behaviors and formats, single-point solutions, and one-and-done actions. We have a tough time organizing for change. Tackling these field-level learning failures is why TLA exists, but I'd challenge all of us to consider what we need to do to learn as richly and effectively as we hope our learners will.

Delivering on a vision for learning that is more personalized and capable of delivering the best for each learner depends on it.

4

The Teaching Job

Brent W. Maddin

I spent nearly two decades betting that better teacher preparation was the key to producing better outcomes for learners. Indeed, I still think that both preservice and in-service training matter immensely. However, I've come to believe that there is something more fundamental to getting better educational results: the way we organize the educator workforce. The one teacher, one classroom staffing model creates a job in which it is nearly impossible for teachers to succeed. More to the point, I'm not convinced that we'll continue to find enough people who will want to be teachers if current trends continue.

The data already reveal the challenges faced by the teaching profession. Teacher preparation programs are facing declining enrollments nationwide, and nearly two-thirds of US parents would not recommend a career in teaching to their children.[1] In addition, younger generations tend toward a greater number of shorter stints in jobs with higher levels of collaboration, and the pandemic catalyzed desire for greater workplace flexibility. Education, long a laggard in workforce innovation, will soon face a reckoning unless there is a serious rethinking of the teaching job.

So, what do we do? For me, the answer lies in building teams of educators with distributed expertise. Notice that I said *educators*, not *teachers*. And while the words *teams* and *distributed expertise* may sound like jargon, they are critical features of a reconceptualized teaching job.

Helping school systems design and implement team-based strategic school staffing models is exactly what I've been up to since 2018 when I founded the Next Education Workforce, an initiative within the Mary Lou Fulton Teachers College at Arizona State University (ASU). We've now worked with nearly one hundred schools across thirty school systems in thirteen states. More than seven hundred professional teachers (and lots of other types of educators) are working on teams that are serving over twenty thousand K–12 learners. Although we are still early in this work, the results across a range of outcomes are promising, and we've learned many lessons along the way.

TEAM TEACHING—HAVEN'T WE SEEN THIS BEFORE?

The idea of team teaching isn't new. It originally rose to prominence as a school reform effort in the United States in the 1960s, but the strategy fell out of favor by the middle of the next decade.[2] Aspects of the practice lived on under various names (such as differentiated staffing and coteaching), but none were as ambitious in scope as the team teaching of the 1950s, 1960s, and 1970s.[3] While the postmortem on last century's teaming isn't complete, a 1973 *New York Times* synopsis of the Ford Foundation's appraisal of its school improvement projects in the 1960s reads: "Team teaching and other staffing changes were discarded not because they lacked promise but because educators were as loath to rearrange their thinking as janitors were to rearrange the furniture."[4]

So why might we expect different results this time around? First, the societal forces are strong. Professionals entering the workforce today crave collaboration, depth over breadth, and flexibility. The current teaching job offers none of that. Second, we are awash in new science-of-learning research and robust data streams that all point to the need for a team with distributed expertise, rather than a single adult, to meet each child's manifold needs. Third, technology, including artificial intelligence, makes some of the technical aspects of implementing team-based staffing easier. Finally, we are seeing a broad coalition interested in redefining the teaching role, including AASA, a national superintendents' association; the national teacher unions; colleges of education; funders; and more than thirty-five of the largest and most influential education organizations.[5]

To be sure, team-based strategic school staffing is a big change, and it's not for everyone. However, in our work at the Next Education Workforce initiative, we've seen this idea take hold and scale across a wide variety of contexts, often at the behest of educators and families. Additionally, we believe that restructuring the educator workforce can help with other transformations of the school system, such as mastery learning and alternative pathways into and through the profession. While these efforts are not the explicit focus of our work, one of the central benefits of the initiative is to open up the possibility for other systems-level reforms.

WHAT EXACTLY ARE TEAM-BASED STRATEGIC SCHOOL STAFFING MODELS?

One of the challenges of working on team-based strategic school staffing is that many educators hear "teams" and think, "We're already doing that." And for good reason. Teams are peppered throughout school environments: grade-level teams, subject-area teams, data teams, school improvement teams, leadership teams, and more. Yes, educators are working together, but rarely do any of these teams require rethinking the teaching job.

At the most basic level, ASU's Next Education Workforce initiative defines team-based staffing models as at least two professional educators sharing a common (and usually larger) roster of learners. Some schools start teaming with a single pair of professional teachers who share the same roster of learners during the same block of time. Although these models are not incredibly *spicy*—a term we use to describe the magnitude of a given model's departure from the status quo—they still confer advantages to both students and educators: content is less siloed, each educator can focus on things they are better at, and the job is less isolating.

We've also seen some schools build teams that comprise all the teachers on a grade level, or even form a couple of mixed-age teams. Spicier models typically consist of a core team of two to four teachers who are joined by other educators for specific times during the day, week, or unit.

The spiciest versions of the strategic school staffing models that we've helped educators design and implement often include three, four, five, and sometimes as many as fifteen educators, including professional teachers working part-time, student teachers, paraeducators in specialized roles, high school students, remote educators, and community educators filling a range of roles including reading tutor, student success coach, and project-based mentor.

Variation Is the Rule, Not the Exception

Each team-based strategic school staffing model looks different. They vary between grade levels, between different schools within the same district, and even within the same grade levels in the same school.

This variation results from differences among the shared student rosters, the curriculum, and the educators. I would design one kind of team if 20 percent of a school's students were multilingual learners engaged in a project-based, interdisciplinary curriculum, with 90 percent of the teachers having fewer than three years of experience. I would design a different staffing model for a school using scripted, high-quality instructional materials, with 60 percent of the students reading significantly below grade level, and with access to four retired elementary teachers to supplement a professional educator staff that perennially has two vacancies.

Given the wide variation in school contexts, my colleagues and I built a framework for strategic school staffing with flexibility at its core. Rather than a prescriptive model, we opted to build a set of design elements. Early on, these design elements were a mishmash of actions taken by educators at different levels within a school system (such as principals providing protected planning time for educator teams or directors of human resources creating new educator roles in the district's HR system). Over time, by studying model designs across dozens of different implementations, we've figured out that the strategic school staffing models have elements that operate at the level of the team, the school, and the school system.[6] All Next Education Workforce team-based models share these elements, but context drives the staffing model design and ultimately what the educator roles look like. Our team collaborates with educators and members of local school communities to design, launch, and scale team-based staffing models that make sense in each particular context, and we offer resources, professional learning, and coaching at every step along the way.

Three Fundamental Shifts

When educators design models grounded in the elements of the Next Education Workforce initiative, we expect to see fundamental shifts in three areas: educators' working conditions; what teaching and learning look like; and how educators enter, specialize, and advance in the profession. Table 4.1 summarizes these shifts.

TABLE 4.1 *Three fundamental shifts when moving from one teacher, one classroom models to Next Education Workforce team-based staffing models.*

Areas of change		*"Old-fashioned" staffing models (one teacher, one classroom)*	*Next Education Workforce team-based staffing models*
Shifts in working conditions	**Number of professional educators**	1; isolated	2–6+; collaborative
	Class size ratios	Constant (25:1)	Variable (100:4; 50:2; 25:1, 5:1)
	Responsibilities	Must be great at everything	Fewer things, more deeply
	Planning time	Typically individual; sometimes collaborative	Protected planning time for team and individual
	Collaboration time	During planning only; outside of instruction	During planning *and* instruction
	Educators' schedules	Inflexible; same most days	Allows for flexibility
	Accountability	For the individual's roster of ~25 students	For the team's shared roster of ~100 students

(continues)

TABLE 4.1 *continued*

Areas of change		"Old-fashioned" staffing models (one teacher, one classroom)	Next Education Workforce team-based staffing models
Shifts in teaching and learning	Instruction	Teacher-centered; siloed, I/we/you; whole class	Learner-centered; interdisciplinary, project-based; small groups
	Student progress	Seat time	Evidence of mastery
	Student outcomes	Narrow, academic	Broader, academic and holistic
	Student-teacher match/ connection	Often based on luck	Better odds of finding an adult with whom a student connects
	Learning space	"My" classroom; inflexible, redundant, underutilized	"Our" learning space; flexible, efficient, choice-filled
	Instructional schedule	Inflexible, shorter blocks, bell-driven	Flexible, longer blocks, educator-driven
Shifts in the ways that educators enter, specialize, and advance in the profession	First year of teaching	Alone, unsupported	On a team
	Responsibilities	All things	Match with level of knowledge and skill
	Approach to hiring	Filling classrooms	Strategic, based on teams' collective expertise
	Professional learning	One-size-fits-all; seat time–based	Personalized and strategic; competency-based
	Advancement	Dead ends; teacher to admin	Pathways; team-level leadership

To get a sense of how these shifts associated with team-based strategic staffing models can impact the teaching job, let's look at a couple of hypothetical educators:

Ms. Adams is a third-grade teacher with fifteen years of experience. She is a great reading teacher but has admitted on occasion that she "isn't really a math person." She is a collaborator and a natural leader who is looking to earn a bit more money and have a greater impact, but she doesn't really want to be an administrator. In the one-teacher, one-classroom staffing model, Ms. Adams is ready to throw in the towel; teaching is just too lonely and requires her to do some things she isn't especially good at, and the job is starting to feel like a dead end.

Mr. Harris *is* a math person. In fact, for the last ten years he worked as an electrical engineer, but he recently moved to a new community and struggled to find work. Although he landed a job as an adjunct instructor of college algebra at the local community college, it was not enough to pay the bills. He is interested in teaching high school math, but he is uncertified and has commitments to the community college on Tuesdays and Thursdays. He admits he is a bit worried about classroom management with high schoolers. Getting an emergency teaching certificate was easy, but in the one-teacher, one-classroom staffing model, finding a school that was interested in him working on a half-time contract proved impossible.

In team-based staffing models, the prospects for Ms. Adams and Mr. Harris are very different. Ms. Adams knows that there will be a lead teacher job opening on the third-grade team, so she will spend her winter break earning three microcredentials in teacher leadership. Not only will the district recognize her personalized professional learning with a modest $150 bump in base pay, she will also be more competitive for the lead teacher position. If she lands the job, she'll make an additional $5,000 a year and lean into her leadership strengths. Notably, she can lead without leaving the classroom. As a member of a four-person team, she'll focus her energy on ELA by planning the reading and writing lessons and using data to deploy the other members of her team—which, in addition to three other teachers, will include five high school reading tutors and three parent volunteers. She'll still teach math, science, and social studies, but she'll never do the lead planning in those subjects.

Mr. Harris can join the faculty at the local high school as a member of a ninth-grade team on a 60 percent contract. This could end up being a perfect fit for him. Although he'll be learning the finer points of classroom management in his alternative certification courses, he'll feel he is developing those skills more quickly because he'll be working so closely with the biology, ELA, and social studies teachers on his team. When Mr. Harris hits a couple of bumps, his teammates will be there to help him out. Together they'll plan interdisciplinary units in which he'll be able to leverage ten years of practical examples from his career as an engineer. Given his Tuesday and Thursday community college commitments, the team will design their schedule such that team-based planning sessions happen on Monday, Wednesday, and Friday, and they'll reserve the other two days for personal planning time.

In our work, we see lots of educators with stories like Ms. Adams and Mr. Harris. Team-based staffing models open up all sort of possibilities for the teaching role that would have been impossible in a one teacher, one classroom setting.

Is Team-Based Staffing Better for Students and Educators?

We know from the history books that one possible reason team teaching didn't survive at scale past the 1970s was a thin evidence base to convince policymakers that these staffing models were good for students and educators. From what research there was at the time, the results were mixed. More recently, Public Impact's Opportunity Culture model—another team-based strategic school staffing model that extends the reach of impactful teachers—has informed our work on how we can leverage other educators to best support student learning. They have been helping districts build strategic school staffing models since 2012; rigorous third-party evaluations show, on average, an extra half-year of learning for students each year.[7] More robust data systems and methodologies, coupled with our increasing ability to measure broader student outcomes like curiosity and sense of belonging, have already helped create a far better evidence base than that from a half century ago.

More than five years into our work, we are starting to achieve enough scale in some school systems to draw inferences of our own. While most of our reach outside of Arizona is still getting off the ground, we are finding promising evidence for an association between team-based staffing models and better outcomes for students and educators in Arizona's largest school district, Mesa Public Schools. Mesa has nearly sixty thousand students and about thirty-five hundred teachers.[8] As of fall 2023, about 20 percent of its teachers were working on teams. All told, about 650 Mesa educators are working on 175 teams serving more than thirteen thousand students in kindergarten through grade 10 across forty-one of Mesa's eighty-three schools.

So, what are we finding? Based on studies conducted by Johns Hopkins University's Institute for Education Policy, the Center on Reinventing Public Education, and ASU faculty, we know that teachers working in team-based staffing models are reporting, on average, statistically significant higher levels of self-efficacy and better relationships with students. They are also more likely to recommend teaching to a friend or family member.[9] Teachers are taking significantly fewer days off, have higher evaluation scores, and are more likely to be retained as teachers in the district in the following year. On average, special educators working in team-based staffing models are particularly satisfied. They are less burnt out, more likely to say they feel respected, and more satisfied with their professional learning.

Student outcomes are also promising. Until a year ago, the data infrastructure did not exist to ask and answer even the most basic questions that involve "team effects." We are only just starting to measure outcomes like sense of belonging and growth of social networks. The first year of academic results suggest that third graders in team-based models are growing an additional 1.5 months in reading, on average, compared with students in traditional staffing models. We have also found that ninth graders served by educator teams are posting five- to seven-percentage-point increases in Algebra I passage rates compared with demographically similar ninth graders in schools with traditional staffing models. We are optimistic about these early results of our work.

We also know there will likely come a time when strategic school staffing will need to defend itself. We should be ready with the receipts. We need to invest more time, energy, and money into studying broader sets of outcomes likely associated with these models using robust, mixed methodologies. That way, when the time comes, we will know with greater certainty that team-based staffing models are unambiguously good for both students and educators.

YES, BUT . . .

Even with promising outcomes, implementing an idea like team-based staffing—which runs counter to one of the most fundamental aspects of traditional schooling—can generate some healthy skepticism that is sometimes immensely difficult to navigate. However, in our experience, the most common misgivings often aren't deal-breakers.

Here are the most common *yes, buts* I have heard while helping build team-based strategic school staffing models across nearly one hundred schools in a dozen states.

Yes, I'm sure this works in Arizona and other right-to-work states, but what about districts with collective bargaining?

The national teacher unions share our concern about the state of the teaching profession.[10] Much of what we advocate for in team-based staffing models is aligned with local unions' priorities, including more educator autonomy, more collaborative planning time, better and more affordable pathways into and through the profession, and evaluations based on a broader set of factors. In addition, as we ensure fair compensation for all teachers, developing more opportunities for educators through differentiated pay for additional roles and responsibilities is another way to strengthen the profession.

Other elements of the teaching profession, some of which the unions have fought very hard for, may need to be reexamined in specific contexts. Class size ratios are an example. In one-teacher, one-classroom models, these ratios are important and relatively easy to calculate. In team-based models, where educators are moving in and out of the learning space and working with highly variable numbers of learners, class size ratio may no longer be a meaningful indicator.

Our conversations with national union leadership have brought out three lessons for any school system contemplating team-based staffing models. First, make sure that teachers are authentically involved in the planning work from the very beginning. For example, educators should be part of the exploration process and initial model design, and they should help to inform the criteria for evaluating whether the shift to strategic school staffing has been a success.

Second, almost every collective bargaining agreement can accommodate strategic school staffing pilots through a memorandum of understanding or other mechanism, and it's in everyone's interest to start small. When school systems start with a handful of intentionally designed pilots and scale at the speed of trust, the educators often become the biggest advocates for a team-based model's expansion.

Finally, if possible, start the work at a time when the collective bargaining agreement is not open for negotiation. When strategic school staffing pilots become part of a negotiation process, it can muddy the overall transformation. If the small, early pilots are successful, the model will spread and naturally become part of the agreement conversations with the support and backing of the educators, administration, and families.

Yes, I can see how your model might work in a newly constructed school with more open learning space, but I'm in a two-hundred-year-old building, and there isn't a single wall that is coming down.

Space and furniture matter. Flexible learning spaces make the job of teaming easier, and the change in environment reminds both educators and students that this isn't business as usual. Unfortunately, changes to the learning space are not always possible. We've come to think about learning space design that accommodates teaming as a continuum, along which there are four levels:

- *Level one.* Leverage existing spaces that are physically close to one another.
- *Level two.* Invest in lower-cost, flexible furniture and/or minor construction.
- *Level three.* Invest in higher-cost, flexible furniture and/or major construction.
- *Level four.* Invest in completely redesigned space or new construction.[11]

About 70 percent of the schools with whom we work fall into level one, but learning teams can do all sorts of things to signal that what used to be four classrooms is now one learning space: no teacher names assigned to any specific room, a strategic allocation of furniture and equipment (such as one classroom library rather than four), and student work displayed across all spaces.

Placing a glass double door between two rooms can have an outsized impact. A lot less costly than removing a wall, glass double doors provide easier movement within the space, flexibility for educators to quickly modify the learning environment, and better lines of sight.

In addition, educators working in teams use other spaces around campus: hallways, media centers, cafetoriums, and football fields may be reserved by educator teams for things like "family meetings" where every educator and learner on a team gather for culture building, whole-group minilessons before moving to differentiated smaller groups, and project-based learning time where students have easy access to educators with distributed expertise. Importantly, most educator teams aren't spending extensive time together with large groups of students. Instead, the educator team groups and regroups students throughout the day to ensure that the right learners have access to the right educators at the right time.

Yes, I can see how these team-based models would be better for both students and educators, but won't it cost a bajillion dollars to implement your "spiciest" model?

It *could* cost a bajillion dollars to build a team-based model with many types of educators, but it doesn't have to. As shown below in table 4.2, the associated costs of the one teacher, one classroom staffing model and a team-based staffing model are comparable. In this example, the team-based model is just $12,000 more expensive. What do we get for that differential? We get a stipend for the lead teacher, a paid teacher resident, two City Year student success coaches, a dedicated special educator, an upskilled paraeducator, a set of project-based mentors, and an annual subscription to AI-based tutoring for every student. Cut one of the student success coaches and the team-based model is $3,000 less expensive than the traditional staffing model.

The example assumes the loss of the salary and benefits of the lowest-paid teacher in the traditional model. The specifics will vary by context, but, before we worry too much about that missing position, we need to acknowledge that many districts have vacancies. Those positions often go unfilled or are staffed by un- or underqualified educators. This may not be the case in every context, and it may be impossible to not hire for a teaching position in some contexts due to district policy or union contracts requiring that all allocated positions based on student enrollment numbers first be filled by credentialed teachers. In that case, other means will be necessary.[12]

There are two additional expenses that the role-by-role cost comparison does not capture. First, it is imperative that educator teams have planning time. For team-based models to work, schools must figure out how to create additional time for teams. They can do so in a variety of ways, including by leveraging community educators to teach high-interest electives while the teachers co-plan, modestly increasing class sizes to create double planning blocks, and relinquishing weekly all-staff meeting time to allow individual teams to meet. For instance, Stevenson Elementary School in Mesa, Arizona, uses several strategies to create more planning time for educator teams. First, the school has built its master schedule to ensure every student shared by a team of educators has specials (art, music, physical education, etc.) at the same time. This creates thirty-plus

TABLE 4.2 *Comparison of approximate costs to staff a one-teacher, one-classroom model and a Next Education Workforce team-based model.*

Traditional Third-Grade Staffing Model	Team-Based Third-Grade Staffing Model
• Four professional teachers, each with 25 students • One special educator (shared across four rooms) • One paraprofessional (shared across four rooms)	• One lead teacher • Two professional teachers • One paid teacher resident • Two student success coaches • Project-based mentors (~1–2 hrs/week) • One digital learning facilitator (dedicated to the team) • One special educator (dedicated to the team) • 100 students

(continues)

TABLE 4.2 *Continued*

1T, 1C Classroom Staffing Model	Cost	Team-Based Staffing Model	Cost
Teacher A (salary $70K, benefits $17.5K)	$88K	Lead teacher (salary $75K, benefits $18.75K)	$94K
Teacher B (salary $55K, benefits $13.75K)	$69K	Teacher B (salary $55K, benefits $13.75K)	$69K
Teacher C (salary $50K, benefits $12.5K)	$63K	Teacher C (salary $50K, benefits $12.5K)	$63K
Teacher D (salary $45K, benefits $11.25K)	$56K	Two student success coaches ($15K each through City Year partnership[a])	$30K
Special educator (salary $60K, benefits $15K) (case load is shared across multiple teachers' classrooms)	$75K	Special educator (salary $60K, benefits $15K) (assumes case load is high enough to associate a 1.0 FTE with single team)	$75K
Paraprofessional (hourly wage plus benefits; shared across four teachers' classrooms)	$20K	Digital learning facilitator (higher than para hourly wage plus benefits)	$23K
		Project-based mentors (partnership with local industry, coordinated by Teacher B)	$0
		Paid teacher resident	$20K
		AI tutors (Khanmigo is $9/mo/ student)[b]	$9K
GRAND TOTAL	**$371K**	**GRAND TOTAL**	**$383K**

[a]City Year charges school districts $150K per year for ten corps members and a coach. See Bill Copeland and Michael E. Raynor, *From Downward Spiral to Virtuous Cycle: City Year's Breakthrough Innovation in Education* (Boston: Deloitte, 2018), https://www.cityyear.org/wp-content/uploads/2019/10/DeloitteWhitePaperSingles _03.2018-1.pdf.
[b]Michelle Cheng, "Every Student Will Have Their Own AI Tutor, According to Khan Academy's Founder," *Quartz*, September 7, 2023, https://qz.com/ai-tutors-for-students-khan-academy-1850807961.

minutes of possible collaborative planning time each day. The district also has two-hour early release on Wednesdays for teacher professional development. Rather than convene the entire staff every week, the principal writes an email with important updates and allows educator teams to use that time to collaborate three of the four weeks each month.

The other expense not captured in table 4.2 involves professional learning. Most successful transitions to these new staffing models require time and training for leaders and educators—whether that is working directly with our team at ASU or carving out the time to do this work during summers, after hours, or during school days, the last of which requires hiring substitutes to cover classes on those days. This costs money, but school systems can often use Title II funds or existing professional development dollars to help offset these costs.

Yes, I can see how team-based models sound very appealing for some teachers, but most of our educators were never prepared to work like this—and some of them won't want to.

Few teachers were initially prepared to work in team-based staffing models. Once they experience it, however, most say they would never go back. That said, getting to that point isn't always easy. Carving out time for educator teams to plan together before the school year starts is imperative to success. Many school systems pay for at least one week of teachers' time during the summer to allow teams to gel, establish norms, and plan the first few weeks of school given a new roster of learners and possibly new teammates.

At the Mary Lou Fulton Teachers College at ASU, we've created a virtual summer institute to help. Educator teams access short, synchronous sessions from ASU and then engage in collaborative worktime with on-demand access to instructors. Session topics include building trust among teammates, identifying the team's collective expertise, and building daily schedules that create flexibility for educators and more deep and personalized learning experiences for students.

In the longer term, the success and scale of team-based models will require changes to teacher preparation programs (some of which are already underway at ASU), where teacher candidates are trained on working in teams and can choose to specialize in particular aspects of teaching. Additionally, ASU creates opportunities for our undergraduate students majoring in education to enter paid roles (such as tutors and digital learning facilitators) in schools with team-based staffing models.

Yes, team-based staffing models sound interesting, but our curriculum, evaluation systems, and data infrastructure are all built around the one-teacher, one-classroom staffing model.

When I started this work, I would not have predicted that one of the biggest challenges to team-based staffing models would be the infrastructure. Student information systems, teacher observation rubrics, and even most project-based learning curricula all assume the one-teacher, one-classroom staffing model. Every school with whom we've partnered has had to figure out workarounds that make team-based staffing models possible within the existing infrastructure.

These infrastructure challenges become a greater problem as the work progresses. Almost every process, procedure, or system can handle a pilot or two. However, when adoption hits a critical mass, more systemic changes must be made.

Student information systems prove to be particularly challenging. These systems play an integral role in school operations including attendance tracking, scheduling, and grading. In traditional staffing models, this work is relatively straightforward: one group of kids, in one classroom, with one teacher, learning one subject during a specific and predictable amount of time. It's easy to see how multiple educators who are dynamically grouping and regrouping students to provide just-right instruction around interdisciplinary content across what used to be multiple classrooms might cause a student information system to throw sparks. Enterprising school administrators have built impressive workarounds, and they are having productive conversations with their student information system providers to create greater flexibility around key variables in the data infrastructure that allow for multiple educators to be associated with a single student during the same time period.

Teacher evaluation and incentive systems must also be addressed. For example, some of our partners are actively redesigning teacher evaluation and pay-for-performance systems to better reflect the shared accountability for student outcomes. Typically, each teacher is evaluated independently based on classroom observations and their students' performance on assessments. In team-based staffing models, it is hard to make inferences about the impact of a single teacher. If the classroom is well-managed and there are two educators in the learning space, should both educators get the same score? Or, if students are learning more by working with five different educators, with which educator should we associate those gains? In most cases, the answers to these questions involve new observation tools to focus on the aspects of teaming and to ensure that accountability for student learning is fairly shared by all educators on the team. These are welcome changes because this sort of spillover influence between educators exists even in traditional staffing models. Team-based staffing models just make it more obvious.

Redesigning educational infrastructure is a lot of work for single school systems to undertake, which is why we are also networking school systems together to put greater collective pressure on infrastructure providers who have little incentive to change.

IS THERE A "SECRET SAUCE" TO CHANGING THE TEACHER JOB?

Educators interested in building team-based staffing models in their local contexts often ask us what's most important to get right. In addition to the challenges and solutions described above, the secret ingredient to team-based staffing, based on our observations of the schools that have tried it, is leadership.

An enthusiastic, mission-aligned, building-level leader is essential. Especially in school systems just starting to redesign staffing models, the leader must be willing to take risks and provide support and cover to educator teams. They must trust the teams to take advantage of their distributed expertise, greater flexibility, and collective autonomy to make the right decisions for their learners.

System leaders must also support this work. As outlined above, there are dozens of structures and systems at the state and local levels that reinforce and reward the one teacher, one classroom model of staffing schools. School systems won't abandon those structures immediately, but, if state and system leaders create the space and conditions for building-level leaders to experiment with staffing their schools, systemwide structures will shift over time.

CONCLUSION

Six years into the work of building team-based staffing models in nearly one hundred schools, I'm more optimistic than I have ever been. I see this work not as one more thing for a school to do, but rather as a paradigm shift in the way that we think about the teaching job and how we staff schools. The future of schooling will almost certainly be more learner-driven, more unbundled, and more likely to value mastery over seat time. I can't think of a better way for schools to be ready for that future than to build teams of educators with distributed expertise who, together, help learners flourish.

5

The Choice Revolution

Adam Peshek

There hasn't been a more important or exciting time to be working on education choice. The years since the COVID-19 pandemic and related school closures have initiated a paradigm shift for millions of families who were forced to take a hard look at routine education arrangements. After decades of experimentation and slow-and-steady progress, education choice is likely to play a much larger role in the future.

If the past few years are an indication of what's to come, the acceleration of education choice will be driven by two elements: First, families and educators are rethinking education by experimenting with new approaches that blur the lines of traditional governance models and frameworks understood by regulators. Second, supportive policymakers are continuing to find ways to unlock funding and break down barriers preventing more families and educators from engaging in these options.

I've focused on education choice for fifteen years as an intern, legislative analyst, lobbyist, policy director, and in vice president roles overseeing policy and advocacy. I have testified in dozens of state legislatures, drafted legislation that became law, and seen some laws I worked on get struck down by courts and others upheld. What I haven't learned on the job or from the many books and articles on the topic over the years, I've learned from the brilliant minds of mentors and colleagues along the way.

Today, I serve as senior director and senior fellow at Stand Together Trust, a national philanthropic organization founded by Charles Koch, where I oversee the organization's work in K–12 education. Our goal is to move education away from a one-size-fits-all approach and toward a bottom-up system defined by education choice, with a dynamic market of education options that are responsive to the needs of children and families. In addition to funding the policy, research, and issue education that has dominated most of my career, the role has afforded me the opportunity to engage in the supply side of education choice—particularly through our support of a burgeoning sector of new school models that have realized significant growth over the past few years.

In this chapter, I'll discuss recent progress on education choice and what I've learned along the way about what has worked and what hasn't. The chapter starts by framing where we are in the education choice movement and then offers six lessons for future reformers. I hope it is helpful to those who want to expand education choice, including lawmakers, policy professionals, and especially early-career advocates who are passionate about the topic and want to make a difference.

WHY EDUCATION CHOICE?

I use the term *education choice* intentionally because the idea of *school choice* is too limiting. Education choice includes private school choice, education savings accounts (ESAs), public school choice, charter schools, homeschooling, course choice, transportation vouchers, part-time school enrollment, course credit for out-of-school learning, dual enrollment, funding for extracurricular activities, and many other variations of choice.

I do not limit the idea to just those activities that are funded or heavily regulated by the government. A family that chooses to homeschool their child is as much a part of the education choice movement as a parent who uses a voucher to enroll their child in a private school or a parent who drives their child across their attendance zone boundary to attend a public school across town.

I believe that parents should be able to make decisions involving their child's education, that students should have more options to pursue in and out of school, and that educators should be treated like professionals who are able to practice their craft in a variety of settings and through a variety of approaches.

This would be an unremarkable statement applied to most other sectors, but in K–12 education, it represents a true paradigm shift. Our system of education was designed with a set of assumptions that were, at best, misguided a century ago and are detrimental today.

The designers of the modern American education system (Mann, Dewey, Thorndike, and many more) deeply distrusted parents, feared the growing number of immigrant and minority populations that could pressure Protestant Anglo majoritarianism, and saw compulsory schooling as a way to socially engineer society.[1] As Horace Mann, father of the common school movement, noted, "Men are cast-iron, but children are wax."[2] Their efforts led us down a path that would treat children like raw materials and schools as efficiently managed factories that would turn those raw materials into specific products.[3]

The faulty assumption of these Progressive Era reformers was that individuals were deviations from the average. In reality, human beings embody what Todd Rose calls "jagged profiles." In his book *The End of Average*, Rose argues that "almost every human characteristic that we care about—including talent, intelligence, character, creativity, and so on—is jagged."[4] There is no mythical model learner, no universal academic motivation, and certainly no average student.

This concept of individual uniqueness and jagged profiles has been a driving force behind my belief in education choice. As Rose notes, "When we are able to appreciate the jaggedness of other people's talents—the jagged profile of our children, our employees, our students—we are more likely to recognize their untapped potential, to show them how to use their strengths, and to identify and help them improve their weaknesses."[5]

I believe we need a dynamic education sector that relies on an expansive supply of education options that best fit the unique needs of students and families. What we had, at least until 2020, was intentionally designed to prevent that from happening.

A MARKET STARTS TO SHIFT

In 2020, every parent of a school-age child was forced to take on more direction and oversight of their child's education. At a minimum, the pandemic required parents to spend more time guiding their children through clumsy and hastily created virtual programs. In the most challenging situations, it required parents to find ways to fill in significant gaps in essential services, such as childcare, therapies for students with disabilities, and meals that children would have received at school if they were attending in person.

In some ways, the pandemic was a nationwide trial of education choice in the US. As with any trial, many participants chose not to renew and returned to traditional schooling as soon as they were able. But for millions of parents, the experience inspired a desire to continue with the alternatives.

What we see today is a shifting market in education with millions of families opting for unique education offerings, a public open to redefining what education looks like, and a political opening that makes big and bold changes a realistic possibility.

A Growing Alternative Sector—Diverse, Boundary Blurring, and Organic

In addition to enrollment increases in schools of choice, families' demand for alternatives can be seen in recent trends in homeschooling. Homeschooling represents the vanguard of the education choice movement in part because it's comprised of the earliest of early adopters: those who are actively directing their child's education themselves, typically with no financial support from the government.

Several analyses—including by the Census Bureau, the *Washington Post*, and the Urban Institute—find dramatic increases in homeschooling enrollment concurrent with an enrollment decline in public schools of more than one million students.[6] Estimated increases in homeschooling since 2019 range from 30 percent to 50 percent, with still sizable 4 to 7 percent increases in private school enrollment figures.

Today, around one in twenty students in the US is homeschooled. This is one of the biggest changes to the American education landscape in decades.

This growth coincides with a demographic diversification of the sector. According to the *Washington Post* analysis, "Home schooling's surging popularity crosses every measurable line of politics, geography and demographics."[7] This sentiment has been echoed in mainstream media coverage, including *PBS News Hour*, CNN, the *Associated Press*, and even an entire episode of *Last Week Tonight with John Oliver* on HBO.[8] The diversity of this new generation of homeschoolers is shattering preconceived notions of what a homeschooling family looks like.

While the term *homeschooling* may conjure the image of children sitting around a kitchen table doing work assigned by their mother, today's homeschooling looks far different. In reality, homeschooling is a catchall term that includes a variety of approaches, including the following:

- *Homeschool cooperatives:* parent-directed organizations that pool resources and expertise to provide group learning environments for homeschool families
- *Microschools:* small schools that resemble twenty-first-century takes on the early American one-room schoolhouse
- *Hybrid homeschools:* schools with characteristics similar to traditional private schools (dedicated educators, facilities, etc.), but attended by students only one, two, or three days per week

These models do not fit neatly into preconceived definitions. The US Department of Education and most states break education into three or four categories: public schools, private schools, charter schools, or homeschools. This categorization masks the nuance that is driving the most innovation in the education market. Hybrid homeschools may look like private schools despite being categorized differently, a homeschool cooperative may include families registered as public school students via a virtual charter school, and microschooling can cut across all sectors.

No one is directing this innovation. Instead, new approaches grow organically to serve family needs. Just as learning pods were cocreated by educators and families looking to regain consistent education during pandemic-era school closures, homeschool cooperatives are being leveraged to create more capacity for homeschool instruction, microschools are proving to help educators implement new ideas, and so forth.

It is no wonder that what these new models are creating lives in the spaces between traditional ideas about governance models.

As these options proliferate, we are witnessing a shift in how parents think about and engage with education options that is completely alien to most education researchers and regulators.

An Openness to Rethinking Education

The growing appetite for significant change can be seen not only through parent behavior (noted above), but also through survey data. Parents are far more open to dramatically rethinking education than ever before.

The "Purpose of Education Index" survey, conducted by Populace, gave parents fifty-seven priorities to rank for their child's education. As the report notes:

> One of the most prevalent threads across the data illustrates that Americans are fed up with the current education system, beyond the point of wanting improvements to the existing structure. Most of the general population believes more things about the educational system should change than stay the same (71 percent), including 21 percent who say nearly everything should change.[9]

Parents also actively prioritize more tailored education experiences for their children, like those that allow children to learn at their own pace and receive unique supports, while deprioritizing one-size-fits-all approaches like standardized tests and a "college for all" push.

A survey of three thousand parents conducted by the consulting firm Tyton Partners reached similar conclusions. In their survey, more than 70 percent of parents expressed interest in exploring new in- and out-of-school options, while a whopping 52 percent of parents indicated a desire to curate their child's education instead of relying on their school system.[10]

A Lack of Confidence in Traditional School Approaches

These shifts in parents' attitudes toward education coincide with increasing frustration with traditional public schools among the general public. In 2023, Gallup found historically low confidence in public schools, with only 26 percent of respondents expressing a "great deal [or] fair amount" of confidence. At a partisan level, only 9 percent of Republicans and 25 percent of Independents expressed confidence, with Democrats still below a majority at 43 percent.[11]

Meanwhile, the public increasingly finds Democrats' ideas on education lacking. Polling from the past twenty years consistently showed Democrats leading Republicans in voter confidence in education, with an average favorability margin of fifteen points. However, Democrats lost voter confidence on education during the pandemic and are at their lowest point in two decades.[12]

A 2022 survey from Democrats for Education Reform reported that 47 percent of respondents said they trusted Republicans to handle public education, compared to 43 percent who trusted Democrats. A separate 2022 survey from the American Federation of Teachers, the nation's second-largest teacher union, showed that Republicans held a one percentage point advantage over Democrats on the issue (39 percent to 38 percent).[13]

But Republicans didn't necessarily gain all the support lost by Democrats. As noted by the American Enterprise Institute's Frederick Hess, while Republicans have seen slight upticks in confidence during the pandemic, their gains are not commensurate with the Democrats' losses. Instead, voters are increasingly distrustful of both parties on education.[14]

This leveled playing field has been seen as a political opening for Republicans to try to lead with messages on education, including education choice. Republican politicians have long been the main *legislative* supporters of private education choice efforts. That's not to ignore the few Democratic political champions—not to mention the wide base of Democratic voters—who express support for education choice. But the inarguable truth is that Republican lawmakers have been the drivers of education choice policy, particularly education choice programs that enable families to fund private education.[15]

This is where we found ourselves during the pandemic: a nationwide crisis with enormous implications for education, a general public open to rethinking education (measured by both actions and sentiment), a loss of trust in the institution of education, and significant changes to political incentives around education. It's within this context that policymakers looked for compelling policy ideas that could be deployed as solutions.

UNIVERSAL EDUCATION CHOICE BECOMES A REALITY

Few policies have been as successful in the education reform space over the past few years as private education choice programs, such as ESAs, tax credits, and vouchers. Instead of the government funding *schools*, these programs fund *students*, and families choose where to direct the funds.

Between 2019 and 2023, after decades of slow and predictable enrollment increases, participation in private education choice programs doubled from 1 percent of students in the country to 2 percent.[16] And that was before several states passed expansive education choice policies, which expanded access to hundreds of thousands of additional students in the 2023–24 school year alone. With this growth, it isn't far-fetched to assume that there will be another doubling of participation in the next few years.

With all this in mind, here are six lessons I have learned while working on education choice. I believe both that these lessons helped secure these recent wins and that they can help keep up this momentum.

LESSONS LEARNED

Lesson One: An Overnight Success Can Take Decades of Work

Only a crisis—actual or perceived—produces real change. When that crisis occurs, the actions that are taken depend on the ideas that are lying around. That, I believe, is our basic function: to develop alternatives to existing policies, to keep them alive and available until the politically impossible becomes the politically inevitable.[17]

These words were written in 1962 by Milton Friedman, the intellectual forefather of the modern education choice movement. But they could have been written sixty years later to describe the recent successes we have seen with education choice campaigns. When the opportunity arose during the pandemic, education choice supporters jumped at the opportunity to pass bold, universally accessible policies.

But these recent successes stand on the shoulders of decades of incremental wins on education choice. In the late 1990s, there were around twenty thousand students participating in private choice programs. A decade later, there were one hundred and eighty thousand. By 2020, that number had jumped to nearly six hundred thousand.[18] It's very likely that more than one million students will be participating in private choice programs in the next few years.

The growth of ESAs is instructive. Instead of limiting funding to sanctioned private schools, ESAs provide families with spending accounts that they can use for private school tuition, tutoring, curricula, extracurriculars, and even homeschooling expenses.

The first ESA program was created in Arizona in 2011 after the state's supreme court struck down two small voucher programs. After Arizona's law stuck, ESA policies grew slowly and steadily for the next decade. A handful of states enacted small programs, some of which were struck down by state courts. But committed advocates persevered, and their determination paid off.

In the 2023 legislative session, seven states enacted new ESA, voucher, or tax-credit programs, and twelve states significantly expanded their existing programs. Data compiled by EdChoice show that between 2021 and 2023 there was a 60 percent increase in access to private education choice. Today, 36 percent of children nationwide—twenty million kids—are eligible for an ESA, voucher, or tax credit for private education. One in five school-age children now lives in a state with a universal education choice program, meaning every child—regardless of income, geography, disability status, etc.—can participate.[19]

We are on the brink of an explosion in participation in these programs. In Florida alone, more than four hundred thousand students are estimated to be enrolled in a choice program after recent legislative expansions.[20]

The slow and steady approach can be frustrating, as any effort full of peaks and valleys can be. But the first thirty years of the movement were crucial to elevating choice as a key policy when the opportunity arose.

During that time, we were organizing coalitions, integrating policies into political platforms, creating administrative infrastructure, studying impact, experimenting with different approaches, and more, to make education choice a reality.

Lesson Learned: Policy movements require a lot of work and time, but it's all crucial in order to prepare yourself for when opportunity knocks.

Lesson Two: Don't Confuse Compromise with an Ideal

Slow and steady progress is a necessary evil, but you should advance bold policies when the opportunity presents itself. I have seen far too many individuals and organizations misunderstand political compromises as an ideal.

The job of advocates is not to pass a watered-down bill in one state, repackage it as a "model policy," and export it across the country. Rather, they should push the limits to get as close as possible to their end goal within the constraints of the *Overton window*—the range of policies deemed acceptable by the public.

When the opportunity presented itself after the pandemic, there were plenty of detractors. Some choice supporters argued then, and now, for a more gradual, phased-in approach that affords regulators and managers more time to wrap their heads around what is happening. They fear that existing programs are growing too large, are too untested, and will lead to a Wild West that is dictated more by supply and demand than by central planners.

This approach is untenable. The charter school movement is a useful example of how compromise can lead to stagnation.

In the 1990s, the charter movement looked much different than it does today—scrappy, zealous upstarts building the sector from scratch. It was a time when scruffy-haired twentysomethings could put together a plan on the back of a napkin and figure it out as they went along. What I hear from many people who were involved with the early charter movement is that it looked a lot like today's growing microschool movement.

Over time, however, the sector did what lots of sectors have done: it accepted rules, regulations, contracts, processes, and many other concessions in the name of quality and risk mitigation. It's death by a thousand cuts. Each new regulation on its face seems reasonable to rein in outlier bad actors. But together, they lead to an environment where those scruffy-haired twentysomethings will never have a shot at turning their idea into a charter school. Today, starting a charter school often requires filling out book-length applications, hiring lawyers, finding political supporters, and procuring million-dollar startup budgets—all before being able to serve a single kid.

Lesson Learned: Advocates need to see the forest for the trees. While compromise is often needed to advance policy, increased regulations should be viewed skeptically and constantly scrutinized in the years after they are passed. Ask yourself if a new regulation is going to make it harder to enter the market, not just whether existing schools can absorb the costs of a new regulation.

Lesson Three: A Policy Is a Means to an End—Not the End Itself

Even more pernicious than embracing compromises is becoming too wedded to a single policy solution. Once you understand your mission (more on that below), this becomes easy to overcome. But too often, individuals and organizations focus too much on a specific policy as if the policy itself were the end goal.

I have been a longtime supporter of ESAs and spent considerable time and effort working on the topic. As a policy advocate and lobbyist, I wrote or helped write many of the early ESA laws. I coedited the first published book on ESAs for the American Enterprise Institute back in 2017.

I support ESAs as a means to an end. ESAs provide students, parents, and educators with the tools (financial, regulatory, and social) to create new and unique learning environments that are responsive to their needs—not the needs of regulators or some vague idea of "society."

But I am more than willing to toss aside ESAs if a better alternative presents itself or if ESAs prove not to achieve the desired end. I am not sure that would have been my position five or ten years ago. It's not appealing to dedicate years to developing expertise in an applied topic only to move away from it when conditions warrant, but that's what is required to stay focused on achieving a *goal* on behalf of kids rather than a *policy win* that might be more about the adults.

For instance, a refundable personal tax credit for education expenses would allow parents to claim a credit on their taxes when they homeschool or send their children to a nonpublic school. Much like the Child Tax Credit or the Earned Income Tax Credit, it could serve as a much simpler approach to education choice that cuts out the middleman.

This ability to adapt helped in Arizona, where advocates were forced to move away from vouchers, leading them to develop ESAs. Arizona's pioneering spirit laid the groundwork for the success of ESAs today. That same mindset can open up new frontiers in school choice in the future.

Lesson Learned: Don't forget that the end goal is not a specific policy. Be willing to drop your preferred policy solution if another one gets you closer to your end goal.

Lesson Four: Sometimes Getting out of the Way Is the Best Way to Help

The education choice movement has spent a lot of time on the demand side, particularly in unlocking dollars and attaching them to families to attend schools of their choice. When it comes to focusing on the supply side, most philanthropic—and even government—efforts focus on replicating existing models. This mentality—along with the death by a thousand cuts via regulations mentioned in lesson two—leads to an environment where very little attention is paid to making it easier to enter the market. In fact, such investment in existing models leads to those supporters *fearing* market-based competition.

In contrast, growth in the number of new small businesses is a key indicator of economic health. Politicians from both parties argue about who better accommodates small businesses. As we do with small businesses, we should pay more attention to the burden of starting a new small school in the education sector.

Part of the plan to help small businesses grow is to lower the barriers to entry. This same plan is needed to ensure that we can support the growing entrepreneurial spirit in educators, who are constantly getting caught up in regulatory fights with city hall on such topics as local zoning ordinances, rules governing how to register as a private school, childcare regulations that often misclassify microschool and homeschool students, compulsory education laws with strict definitions about the number of days and hours that schooling is required, and much more.

In Arizona, a potential microschool founder signed a contract on a two-acre property and paid a nonrefundable deposit, only to be stopped by zoning officials who informed her that schools need to be on a minimum of five acres.[21] In Nevada, a retired Navy officer and trained engineer was unable to open a private microschool because state law requires a state teacher's license (a requirement waived for *religious* private schools).[22] A health department in southern Nevada wouldn't allow a microschool to order pizza for students on Fridays because it lacked a commercial kitchen.[23] Prospective microschool founders have been told that they violate zoning regulations because they are a "business, not a school;" ordered to install elevators to comply with the Americans with Disabilities Act; and even required to register as a daycare and forced to set up diaper-changing stations even though their school teaches teenagers.[24]

These are just a handful of the hundreds of examples I have seen from all corners of the US that impede entrepreneurial educators from launching new schools.

Lesson Learned: Education entrepreneurs in every state are dealing with bureaucratic regulations. If we care about increasing the number of seats and growing the number of entrants in the market, then we need to focus on the real barriers that are preventing them from serving more students.

Lesson Five: The Customer Is the End User

If there is a lesson that has been learned time and time again, it's that programs are more likely to fail because of poor implementation than poor policy design. In the case of ESA programs, they are not most likely to fail because of lack of parent demand—they are most likely to fail because advocates and regulators are making them painfully difficult to use.

I once believed in the potential of online marketplaces to implement ESA programs. As mentioned, in 2017 I coedited a book on ESAs and wrote a chapter that focused on the future of implementation. In it, I promoted the idea of online marketplaces as a way to make it easier for parents to purchase curriculum, instructional materials, consumables, and other purchases not as easily automated as tuition or tutoring. Instead of archaic systems consisting of submitting receipts and forms and hoping to get your reimbursement check weeks later, I argued that an online system that allowed parents to direct funding to providers in real time would provide the sort of streamlined process we want.

Now, I believe those systems are doing more harm than good in the effort to provide families with more educational options. Allow me to offer a mea culpa for my blind spot.

While online marketplaces and platforms have become the standard approach in the nascent world of ESA implementation, their execution has been botched. Somewhere along the way, some ESA administrators have misinterpreted their role as being a procurement depot, which transforms them from enablers into barriers.

ESA administrators and the governments that contract them have mistakenly assumed that they need to create marketplaces where all vendors, payments, expenses, and other items need to be uploaded and sent through layers of bureaucratic approval before being executed. Whether it is a $1 notepad or a $1,000 tuition payment, the same levels of scrutiny apply.

The government is not good at creating functioning markets, but it is very effective at stepping in to make it harder for supply and demand to meet. I've come to believe that the first order of business should be to enable parents and education providers to make transactions in a streamlined way—whether through a debit card, ACH transfers, or some other method—instead.

Lesson Learned: Over-engineered solutions are usually designed for people other than the end user. Before you create a solution in search of a problem, it's best to keep it simple and build as you go based on the feedback provided by the consumer. Before you add layers of complexity and grow a government apparatus to navigate that complexity, realize that it will likely hamstring the growth and usability of these programs.

Lesson Six: Understand the Audience You Are Trying to Reach

When it comes to adopting new ideas or products, there is always an adoption curve. It starts with innovators, then goes through early adopters, early majority, late majority, and finally the laggards.[25] The innovators and early adopters need little convincing—they see the benefit of the policy or product and jump in. The early majority are open but skeptical and need to understand how it will benefit them. The late majority need to see most people adopting the behavior before jumping in. Laggards, at the end of the curve, will be the last to adopt and embrace an idea—and will spend most of their time throwing metaphorical rocks at it.

I have seen the education reform community spend a lot of time trying to make the late majority and laggards like their ideas. They obsess over the talking points and policy language needed to convince the suburban mom in a million-dollar home that her zoned blue-ribbon public school isn't as good as she thinks. Or they'll spend years of their lives arguing with those who support test-based accountability about why the benefits of pluralism outweigh marginal improvements in math and reading scores. They will try to convince a regulator that regulations are counterproductive.

These audiences will not be moved; they will just throw rocks at your idea while prefacing each lob with, "I support education choice, but . . . ." There are many education reformers who proclaim themselves supporters of school choice, but who are ultimately not comfortable with parents making decisions without expert input.

Here is a typical exchange of circular reasoning:

LATE MAJORITY SKEPTIC: "The wealthy are using learning pods while schools are closed, and it's going to drive inequalities."

EARLY ADOPTER: "Let's give the poor some money so they can afford to do learning pods too."

LATE MAJORITY SKEPTIC: "We can't unlock funding to let the poor access learning pods until we can evaluate whether they will be learning."

My advice is to move on from there. There are huge untapped populations of individuals and groups who are naturally sympathetic to our solutions: homeschool families, proponents of unconventional education approaches, young families with kids who are not yet school-age, families who seek out public school open enrollment options, and others who are clearly open to joining the effort. My advice is to seek out these audiences in order to build new constituencies to further expand education choice.

Lesson Learned: It is enticing to think that a well-constructed argument will transform the way a choice opponent thinks. In reality, you'll make far better use of your time by focusing on the individuals who are more sympathetic to the idea. Skeptics will only be moved by social proof, and to create social proof, you need to focus on a movable audience.

CONCLUSION

These are just a handful of hundreds of lessons I've learned in my time focused on education choice, but they are among the most important to share at this important juncture in the movement. After nearly four decades of slow and steady growth, recent policy victories have laid the groundwork for an explosion in participation from families. For decades, education reformers dreamed of a day when parents would take more control of their child's education, when educators would be open to bucking the status quo, and when lawmakers would be incentivized to enact big and bold education choice legislation. That day is here. The question is whether we can push further to make education choice a consistent feature of the American education system for centuries to come.

6

School Size

Michael Q. McShane

One word. Five letters.

If there has been one single word that has shaped thinking about educational innovation and improvement over the course of the past two decades, it has been *scale*. The scale of the problems in education in America is enormous, so the scale of the solution (or solutions) must also be enormous.

How to scale reforms has been the subject of research initiatives, philanthropic giving, and federal grant dollars. When the Brookings Institution launched an entire project dedicated to scaling education interventions, scholars Larry Cooley, Maud Seghers, and Jenny Perlman Robinson wrote in a February 2021 blog post: "Given the mismatch between massive educational challenges and resources that are stretched paper thin, it is essential to make the most out of every dollar invested by parents, schools, NGOs, and governments. . . . The education field is littered with impactful efforts that, at best, remain islands of excellence and, at worst, cease to exist."[1]

Scale has been a key goal of most of the major education funders in America, as well. In a 2011 monograph outlining their investment strategy, the Bill & Melinda Gates Foundation wrote, "Our goal is to help [grantees] create tools that can scale easily and that substantially increase the number of college- and career-ready students."[2] The Walton Family Foundation education program's website states explicitly that the organization "support[s] new ideas that have a measurable impact on student success. And we tailor and scale what works."[3] In the spring of 2021, LaVerne Evans Srinivasan, vice president of the Carnegie Corporation of New York's National Program and its program director for education, wrote, "We have the proof points and know-how to transform learning, bolster instruction, and meet the needs of our most disadvantaged students. What has changed is the urgency for doing so at scale."[4]

The federal government has gotten in on the scale game, as well. The federal Charter Schools Program, initially formulated as part of the 1994 reauthorization of the Elementary and Secondary Education Act and expanded in 1998, "administers discretionary grants that support the startup of new charter schools and the replication and expansion of high-quality charter schools."[5] And the Investing in Innovation grant program—part of the 2009 American Recovery and Reinvestment Act—was launched to support and research promising innovations in education with the hope that successful ones could scale. In both cases, the federal government was not looking to support small, organic interventions.

BIGGER ISN'T ALWAYS BETTER

Scale, then, has been the watchword for education reform. But an insurgent movement has developed in recent years. Rather than trying to find solutions that serve huge numbers of students, the movement is focused on creating learning environments that serve just a few students—as evidenced by trends in microschooling, homeschooling, and tutoring.

Microschooling

Microschools, as their name might suggest, are purposefully small schools that often cap enrollment at fifteen or twenty students. The Prenda schools, which started in Yuma, Arizona, are one example. Prenda schools meet in homes, public libraries, and other nonconventional spaces. Students are not age-graded into classrooms but work both independently and collaboratively at tasks geared toward their level of learning and interests.

When the coronavirus hit, Prenda and other microschools were in a strong position. Because the schools were so small, it was easier to keep up with social distancing guidelines. There were fewer students who could bring the virus into the classroom. And, if a student was exposed, they could do much of their academic work from home. But more than that, microschools became small communities with high levels of trust where adults and children were working together and supporting each other. In times of trial, trust and communal bonds are key. Prenda schools had these bonds at the beginning of the pandemic, allowing them, and many other microschools, to expand or open in the years since.

Homeschooling

Homeschooling has also grown substantially since the onset of the pandemic. A *Washington Post* analysis from October 2023 examined states' homeschooling figures and found a 51 percent increase in homeschool enrollment across the country from 2017–18 to 2022–23. In their words, "Home schooling's surging popularity crosses every measurable line of politics, geography and demographics. The number of home-schooled kids has increased 373 percent over the past six years in the small city of Anderson, S.C.; it also increased 358 percent in a school district in the Bronx."[6]

Homeschooling suffers from inaccurate stereotypes, like the idea that homeschooled children are isolated in their own homes and learn solely with and from immediate family members. Researchers Albert Cheng of the University of Arkansas and Daniel Hamlin of the University of Oklahoma analyzed the 2012, 2016, and 2019 administrations of the federal National Household Education Survey (NHES) and found 1,468 respondents who identified as homeschoolers. They were able to use questions in the NHES to analyze homeschooled children who are taught by private tutors or belong to a homeschooling cooperative: between 45 and 52 percent of respondents said that they used a private tutor or belonged to a homeschool cooperative.[7]

Looking at monthly EdChoice polling from June 2022 to July 2023, a consistent two-thirds of parents indicated that they were either "very favorable" or "somewhat favorable" toward homeschooling, while only a third said that they were "not that favorable" or "not at all favorable."[8] According to the 2023 Schooling in America Survey (also conducted by

EdChoice), 14 percent of American parents said that they would home-school if money and logistics were no obstacle.[9]

Tutoring

In the wake of the coronavirus pandemic, tutoring has emerged as a strategy for learning recovery. Of course, tutoring is not new. For generations, wealthier families have utilized tutoring to help their children in classes in which they are struggling or to enrich the learning that they are receiving. Schools have also utilized tutoring (often in piecemeal and ad hoc ways) at various times and in various places to try to improve student learning outcomes. In a poll from September 2023, 40 percent of American parents said that they were either currently utilizing tutoring for their child, were looking for a tutor, or planned to look for a tutor in the near future. They indicated that they would spend, on average, $369 per month to hire one.[10]

Before we get to the future of small learning environments, it is worth heading at least briefly back to the past to understand why schools are the size that they are today. In fact, the young people being tutored today have something in common with one of the greatest military leaders in human history.

A BRIEF HISTORY OF SCHOOL SIZE

For centuries—if not millennia—small learning environments have been the preferred model for elites. Aristotle tutored Alexander the Great at the behest of Alexander's father, Philip II of Macedon. Isabella of Castille instructed her four daughters at home in the fifteenth century. Those women would go on to become the queens of Portugal, the Netherlands, and England, and would help spread the Renaissance across the European continent.[11] In more recent times, best-selling author and successful podcaster Rory Stewart worked as a tutor for Princes William and Harry while he was a student at Oxford.[12]

The problem for everyone else has been financial and logistical. Small learning environments are labor intensive; labor is expensive; therefore, small learning environments are expensive. As America became engaged in the Common School movement in the mid-nineteenth century, schools had to become bigger to accommodate the goal of universal access. Not every child could be provided bespoke tutoring in the home. These economies of scale have persisted over time and helped instigate, starting in the late nineteenth century, the consolidation of schools and districts in America.

The early twentieth century saw the birth of the comprehensive high school. In 1918, the National Education Association–appointed Commission on the Reorganization of Secondary Education published a report that shaped what high schools in America look like to this day. It identified seven cardinal principles for high schools: health, command of fundamental processes, worthy home membership, vocation, citizenship, worthy use of leisure, and ethical character. It argued for both specialization and unification. As George Copa and Virginia Pease described it, "Specialization was to occur through a curriculum differentiated by vocation (e.g., agriculture, business, clerical, industrial, fine arts, household arts, and academic). Unification was to be accomplished by housing the students under one roof and requiring a series of constant subjects for all students."[13]

This became the organizing principle for public schools. The existing patchwork of small districts, often operating single-site K–12 schools that had dotted the American landscape, amalgamated into a smaller set of larger districts, often anchored by its comprehensive high school. Between 1940 and 1980, over one hundred thousand school districts were eliminated, with the average number of districts per state dropping from 2,437 to only 318 and the number of pupils per district growing from 216 to 2,646.[14]

Why did this happen? A full explanation is beyond the reach of this chapter, but the central explanation is that many more young people started to attend high school, and its goals started to shift from strictly college preparation to preparation for both college and work immediately after graduation. As Nobel Prize–winning economist Claudia Goldin explained:

> The demand for educated labor in the United States increased, and almost nationwide there was an outpouring of public and primarily local resources to build and staff high schools. These schools were academic (not industrial), free, secular, gender neutral, open, and forgiving. The education

change was known then as the high-school movement. . . . In 1910 just one American youth in ten was a high-school graduate. By 1940, the median youth had a high-school diploma.[15]

The large, comprehensive school emerged at a particular time to solve a particular set of problems. Putting as many young people as possible under one roof to offer them both a common experience and a wide set of potential courses and activities was a reasonable, and, as Goldin and others have argued, incredibly effective way of reforming the educational environment for that day and age.

Zoom forward to early 2023, when a short TikTok video tour of Carmel High School in suburban Indianapolis went viral. Created as part of a career and technical education club project, the video (and a second follow-up) showed all of the amenities available to the school of nearly fifty-five hundred students. More than thirty-four million viewers saw the school's bookstore, auto shop, jewelry room, massive football stadium, café and market, TV and radio studios, swimming facilities, ceramics rooms, esports room, and more.[16] Like most things that went viral, it stoked controversies about school spending and the racial makeup of the school, but the lasting impression that one gets from watching the video is simply the sheer size of the endeavor.

Carmel is an outlier, but it illustrates the reality that larger schools can offer a wide range of activities and environments. This is because huge amounts of funding follow those students into the school, and enough students will be there to support everything from sports teams and bands to arts programs and shop classes.

A NEW (OLD) PARADIGM

It is worth asking if the same constraints and benefits that led to school consolidation still exist, and whether the large, comprehensive high school remains the best way to prepare students for adulthood.

Despite the benefits that modern high schools like Carmel offer, for some—perhaps many—students, they are too big and impersonal. And, as the future of work and the requisite skills and talents become more nebulous and uncertain, the logic of batch-processing large numbers of students through a standardized program of study makes less and less sense. As social media and other technological advances atomize and alienate young people, it clarifies the need for more tight-knit communities. It is tough to do that when the community comprises thousands of young people.

John Dewey, the ideological lodestar of the Progressive Era that brought us large schools, famously argued, "What the best and wisest parent wants for his child, that must we want for all the children of the community. Anything less is unlovely, and left unchecked, destroys our democracy."[17] The best and wisest parents (to borrow Dewey's language) have looked to smaller learning environments for their children for ages and, as polling data suggests, continue to drive parental interest in these options today.

So what is different now from when the constraints of scale led to consolidation a century ago?

Technology

As it has in so many other areas of society, technology is starting to change the equation on learning.

Before, almost all of the technological advances in education pushed people into larger and larger shared spaces. Whether it was chemistry labs or overhead projectors, technology made teaching large groups of people in a single space easier and more effective. Schools were built around gyms, auditoriums, labs, workshops, and libraries, and they acted as a repository and organizer of these technologies. It made sense to require students to attend those specific places for a particular amount of time so that they could access the resources made available to them by tax dollars.

Now, Prenda, mentioned earlier, uses learning management software to provide math and English language arts instruction to students. While students are together physically in their microschool, they work independently—often online—on content specifically targeting their educational needs. In addition, the more group-oriented and non-technology-based projects are curated centrally by Prenda and distributed to guides so that they don't have to find projects for all of their students individually. Students are able to choose projects from the central repository. This ensures that what they *are* doing is aligned with what they are *supposed to be* doing, while still allowing for a degree of personalization for their interests and needs. All of these things make the job of teaching easier and allow a single guide to manage the education of a dozen or more students, which makes the financial model work—if, as you'll see soon, barely.

Changes in Work Habits and Norms

Before, more standardized work arrangements made it easier for schools to sync children's schedules with their parents'. By starting school roughly an hour before the typical workday started, parents had time to get their children to school before heading to the office or the factory. And while there was often a gap between dismissal and the end of a shift, afterschool activities could fill that space. The custodial element of education—that is, that schools were a safe place for kids to be out of the house for six or seven hours a day—was key.

Now, polling data tell us that schooling models with alternative schedules and calendars are popular with parents. As part of our regular polling on education issues, EdChoice has asked the following question to a representative sample of American parents every month since January 2021: "In order to provide the best education for your child/children, what would be your preferred weekly schedule and location between schooling at home with a parent/teacher/tutor, or outside the home?" Parents' responses have been consistent. Between 10 and 15 percent of parents have stated that they would like to educate their child entirely at home. Between 40 and 50 percent of parents have stated that they would like to educate their child entirely outside the home, and between 40 and 50 percent of parents have said that they would like some kind of hybrid schedule with students learning from home between one and four days per week.[18]

Hybrid homeschooling offers a midway point between large and small, enrolling students in a traditional learning environment for part of the week, but having them work in a small, home-based environment for the rest of the week. Many hybrid models have students spend more time out of the home as they age—so small children might spend four days at home and only one day at school, while high school students spend four days at school and one at home. Given the flexibility enjoyed by many families in their work schedules and the flexibility exhibited by innovative school leaders, learning environment size does not actually have to be either large or small.

Changes in Funding Philosophies

Looking back at the way philanthropy has approached educational innovation, it is hard not to be reminded of the 2005 volume *With the Best of Intentions: How Philanthropy is Reshaping K–12 Education*, and particularly the chapter by Jay Greene entitled "Buckets into the Sea." Greene observed that the $1.2 billion that the nation's education philanthropies were spending at the time paled in comparison to the $427 billion that the K–12 education system spent. He argued that if philanthropies were going to be such a small part of the total spending in the nation, they would have to focus on higher-leverage giving.[19]

Greene specifically used the example of small schools to illustrate his point. He wrote, "Once a small public school is created with private money, it will be supported far into the future by public operating dollars because of the per-pupil revenue generated by each public school student who attends the small school."[20] He analogized this giving model to "building a channel through which the ocean will flow. Once you finish the private effort of digging, the ocean of public dollars will move on its own in this new direction."[21] This idea—that philanthropic giving is better off *either* trying to influence public policy in ways that redirect the vast amount of public spending *or* creating institutions that are funded by that vast amount of public spending—supercharged discussions of scale. It also allowed philanthropists to think of solutions that would serve millions or tens of millions of students, rather than the hundreds or thousands for whom they had previously supported solutions.

Perhaps the most interesting new philanthropic organization on the scene is the VELA Education Fund, which launched as a joint project of the Walton Family Foundation and the Charles Koch Institute in 2019.[22] To date, it has awarded more than twenty-five hundred small grants to emerging educational entrepreneurs. Its three grant programs—valued at $2,500 to $10,000 for the first step, $50,000 for the intermediate step, and $250,000 for models pushing toward wider adoption—are designed to support ventures at various early stages.

VELA grants money to three different types of entrepreneurs: those who are building unconventional learning environments, those who are building products or services to help the building of unconventional learning environments, and "community catalysts" who help increase access to such environments. They accept applications over a rolling period throughout the year and endeavor to get money to entrepreneurs quickly, without forcing them to jump through onerous hoops or complete unnecessary paperwork.

It is hard to understate how different this model is from the vast majority of philanthropic giving in education. The question, "Can it scale?" is not part of the decision criteria for VELA's giving, at least in its initial phases. If a new learning environment only exists to serve a small number of students, VELA deems supporting that perfectly acceptable. What's more, their grantmaking process recognizes that small organizations do not have the same ability to complete massive amounts of paperwork, making it less biased against small, upstart entrepreneurs. VELA is just one example of how today's philanthropic giving can lead to more small learning environments.

Changes in Public Funding

Before, small learning communities had to be funded directly by parents out of their own pockets. This meant that such options were the sole purview of the affluent or those who were able to make in-kind contributions like volunteering to teach or work off the cost of educating their child.

Now, efforts to supersize these smaller school environments have been catalyzed by major recent developments in one crucial area: public policy. Since 2021, Arizona, Arkansas, Florida, Iowa, Utah, and West Virginia have created universal or near-universal education savings account programs, which will place public funding into a flexible-use spending account that parents can spend on private education providers. Whereas previous generations of private school choice programs, such as vouchers and tuition tax credits, assumed a traditional school organization and that the scholarship would be spent entirely on one provider (a traditional school), these new models allow for much more flexibility. School size is one of the dimensions in which that flexibility can be exercised. Unlike the days of Alexander the Great—or even America's early elite—families who would not otherwise have the means to act on their preference for small learning communities can now do so.

MORE POSSIBLE THAN EVER, BUT STILL NOT EASY

Up to this point, this chapter has been quite bullish on the prospect of small, alternative learning environments. But their future is far from certain. Small schools face some serious challenges that are worth examining, including an uncertain business model and political pushback. These issues are the most commonly cited when I talk to the leaders and families who have been at the forefront of the small school movement.

The Business Model

The most pressing concern for the fledgling alternative education community is the basic unit economics that anyone with a pencil, a sheet of paper, and a calculator can compute.

Let's put together a fictional microschool. First, we would need a location. In my old neighborhood in Kansas City, rent for a simple storefront will run between $15 and $20 per square foot per year, so a fifteen-hundred-square-foot space will run between $22,500 and $30,000. You want a great teacher or guide? The starting salary for Kansas City Public School teachers is $43,100.[23] Public school teachers get tens of thousands more in health-care and retirement benefits, but even assuming just a 15 percent benefit cost brings the teacher to just under $50,000. You need insurance, utilities, furniture, and other incidentals, which could easily crack another $1,000 to $1,500 per month. Add in instructional materials, as well as any educational technology, and even with some pretty careful assumptions, you're in the range of $85,000 to $100,000 per year.

There are steps that small school founders can take to keep costs down. Some schools start in the founder's home. If more space is needed, renting space rather than buying it can allow providers to pass maintenance expenses onto a landlord instead of having to foot the bill themselves. Renting can also allow for much more flexibility to move if a cheaper alternative becomes available or if the school grows beyond what its current space can hold. Plus, renting allows schools to use nontraditional spaces that they might be able to get a deal on. Those who rent can look to space owned by a church or nonprofit, which could offer school leaders a below-market rate. But partnerships are tricky. Education entrepreneurs are replete with stories of getting space donated or offered at a discounted rate only to have the rent increased when the landlord discovers that they are making money.

Another way to drive down costs is to rely on donated time. School founders who serve as the guide or teacher themselves can discount their own time or educate their own children as a way to bring down the cost. The school might also create its own curriculum or educational resources from free sources available online or in the community. Parents can work as teachers or can help out in other ways at the school (from doing bookkeeping to cleaning) rather than hiring someone to do that work. But, as with donated space, teacher-founders with their own children in the school bring a host of troublesome relational, personal, and financial entanglements. There is no such thing as a free lunch.

Getting great teachers could be a challenge as well. In the hypothetical above, we budgeted for the starting salary of a teacher. But teachers with more experience will expect more money, and great teachers will want to be paid a premium as well. In many of the new school models, teachers are hourly employees without the same security and benefits of traditional employment.

Small learning environments generally offer teachers a different value proposition than traditional employment. While they cannot always compete on salary (though some microschool networks are trying to make higher salaries work), microschools are offering vastly superior working conditions. Working in a traditional school subjects teachers to all sorts of emotional distress. Teachers may be working in large, unfeeling communities; teaching boring curricula; dealing with misbehaving students and parents who work against rather than with them; and finding few opportunities for creativity and professionalism. On the other hand, the smaller learning environments I've been describing promise opportunities for teachers to do engaging things like designing lessons, working with students one-on-one, and more—and to experience less of the drudgery along the way. They are banking that it's worth money.

While many appreciate the flexibility and want to work part-time, it is a much tougher sell for someone trying to make teaching a career. Lots of frustrated teachers or former teachers are attracted to these models, and there are parents who are interested in working part-time. The question is whether there are enough.

This is particularly true for ventures that look to recruit top teacher talent, offer innovative learning spaces, or use the latest technology to supplement instruction. Small learning environments may be able to cut costs by purchasing in bulk, using tech for some efficiencies, using free learning materials, or relying on in-kind contributions for space. But the basics of location and personnel are inflexible and cost the most money.

Venture capitalists see an opportunity to make money. The microschool network Primer has raised $18.7 million in venture funding—including a Series A round led by Keith Rabois of Founders Fund, known for his work with PayPal and LinkedIn as well as early investments in YouTube and Airbnb. Prenda has raised $45.9 million over eight rounds of venture finance. Sora, another network, has raised $23.5 million. Kaipod Learning, another microschool organization, was selected for the prestigious Y Combinator accelerator. These private investors clearly see an opportunity for profit, but what exactly that opportunity will look like remains unclear.

The Political Pushback

Finally, there are political challenges to go along with political opportunities. Pandemic learning pods were slammed as inequitable because they would exacerbate learning gaps between students with and without access to higher-quality online learning.

Back in 2020, for instance, the *Wall Street Journal* published an opposition report on Prenda microschools put together by the National Education

Association, the nation's largest teacher union.[24] It admitted that micro-schooling had "widespread support" and offered the backhanded compliment that they might expand opportunity gaps (because the schools were so good that they would likely exacerbate inequality). But, most troublingly, it contained a picture of founder Kelly Smith's house and his address, along with a strategy to stop Prenda's growth. As new models expand and grow, the target on their back will grow as well. The teacher union playbook against charter schools—smear all schools with the scandals of one school or network, claim that they are "draining" funds or aren't fully accountable, etc.—can be run just as easily against these new models.

WHAT IF SCALE WERE THE FRIENDS WE MADE ALONG THE WAY?

It would be a bit rich if purposefully small educational models became the education solution that actually scaled to meet the significant challenges of the American education system. If several of these venture capital–backed models can open thousands or tens of thousands of microschools, or if millions of families are able to find ways to sustain homeschooling, it might teach us an interesting lesson about what leads to scale in American education.

What if scale occurs organically from the bottom up rather than from the top down? What if scale cannot be managed cleanly and only emerges chaotically and in ways that aren't easily observable? In some ways, this would echo the chaotic and organic growth of schooling in America prior to the Common Schools movement, when hundreds of thousands of small schools and districts emerged to meet the needs of fledgling communities. It was only after this foundation was created that anyone tried to organize and rationalize it into a system of education.

What if this is just the historical pendulum swinging back, as it tends to do? Schools were too small, chaotic, and decentralized to meet the needs of the growing industrial economy. So they became larger and more standardized and centralized. Now, schools have become too rigid and centralized for the diverse, pluralistic population of our nation and the wide range of jobs and life paths available to students upon graduation. So the return to smaller, less centralized, and more diverse schooling could be where education is headed.

It would seem that slow, organic growth is a recipe for institutions that can last. The constraints of the past—whether driven by society, economics, policy, or practice—have changed, and schools are able to change along with them. Entrepreneurs have engaged in a tremendous amount of creative problem solving and have offered a variety of different ways to organize learning environments.

When change happens centrally, at scale, and from the top down, a new school board or legislature or governor can scupper everything that the previous lot built and do something completely different. The roots of change are shallow and the soil dry. But if change is the result of thousands or even millions of small decisions that no one person or institution managed, the roots can grow much deeper into richer soil. Paradoxically, the path to scale might not be aiming for it immediately, but rather nurturing numerous smaller attempts to create great learning environments, some of which might scale and some of which might not. But it is the sum total of all of those efforts that will create the scale to affect meaningful positive change in the American education system.

7

Unleashing a Movement for Profession-Based Learning

Corey Mohn

Sitting at Roasberg, a quaint coffeehouse in the city center of Helsinki, Finland, I find myself with *windshield time*—idle time during travel—pondering the current state of our education system and the idyllic version awaiting us on the other side of enlightenment. There is a yawning gap between what is and what could be.

The other thing I'm experiencing today at Roasberg is the number of trams that pass the front window. I have a view of one of the busiest corridors in the country and, in the past hour, I've counted thirty-eight tram crossings, an average of one every ninety-five seconds. But none of the locals here seem to notice. This constant buzz of trams appears to be so much a part of daily life as to fade into the background for them.

While counting trams is diverting from the task at hand (writing this chapter), the fact that the Finns are oblivious to the trams is a metaphor for how many of us in the K–12 education system operate. How many times have we let the routine operations of our systems become invisible, such that they are no longer top of mind when we consider what we can add, what we can remove, and what can evolve or otherwise change? We assume that some things are absolute truth and therefore immovable.

I find myself in Helsinki because HundrED, a global, mission-driven organization that works to identify, amplify, and facilitate the implementation of impactful and scalable education models, is hosting a summit to celebrate the top one hundred global innovations in education. My organization, the Center for Advanced Professional Studies (CAPS) Network, is receiving this designation for the second straight year. Being around educators and entrepreneurs from forty-seven different countries over three days, you cannot help but wonder: how much is our view of what is possible skewed by systems that have become so routine that they are almost invisible?

ABOUT THE CAPS MODEL

CAPS is a profession-based learning program for high schools designed to support students in building skills and knowledge in the context of real challenges faced by organizations in their communities. Students work across numerous industries, such as health care, engineering, global business, bioscience, creative media, technology, teacher education, and beyond. They work with and are mentored by professionals. And they learn to be comfortable and confident with experimentation—leveraging any failure as a growth opportunity. Needless to say, CAPS is not the typical high school experience.

Its story begins in 2006, when Blue Valley—an extremely high-performing public school district in Kansas—made the surprising decision to diversify its offerings to improve relevance, not just rigor. Located in the suburbs of Kansas City, the Blue Valley School District began creating a program that is in many ways antithetical to the No Child Left Behind mentality dominant in the first decade of the new millennium. (No Child Left Behind, a federal law enacted in 2002, aimed to improve K–12 education by emphasizing accountability and standardized testing. It required schools to meet annual proficiency targets, with consequences for those failing to do so.) Then-superintendent Dr. Tom Trigg worked with a school board consisting primarily of business executives from the community to reimagine learning, shifting from one-size-fits-all test and college prep to relevant, authentic, and real-time experiences.

With the launch of Blue Valley CAPS in the fall of 2009, Blue Valley made a bold statement: for our students to be successful in life, we need to bring them context that matches the content.

But as mentioned above, Blue Valley was a successful district prior to launching CAPS. As a former superintendent once told me, "Blue Valley won No Child Left Behind." Indeed, assessment scores for the students of the district were at the top of nearly all national ratings. So why change course?

The decision for Blue Valley Schools to create CAPS was made at the confluence of interests of industry partners, parents, and students. When asked what skills, attributes, and actions were required for a young professional to be successful, industry partners in the community related a desperate need for students to obtain durable skills such as effective communication and time management. Parents in the district noticed a lack of confidence and certainty in their child's direction heading into a postsecondary institution or first job. Students made clear they were hungry for more opportunities to explore areas of interest and lead their own learning.

This is not to say that all parents and students were immediately on board with this dramatic change of approach. Tension existed in the early years of the program, particularly with high-achieving students looking to drive up their GPA and class rank, which they deemed a surer strategy for future success. But as students experienced the new program, most skeptics changed their tune.

The CAPS model immerses students in a professional culture. Blue Valley CAPS students participate for nearly half their school day, every day, with the program complementing core learning at a comprehensive high school.

Actual employers mentor students as they navigate their journeys of self-discovery. Over the course of a semester, students either validate their love of a career trajectory or reject it, known within CAPS as *Try it out; rule it out*. Unlike at many traditional career academies, at CAPS, a student ruling out an industry is given a soft off-ramp and the ability to begin exploring another field without penalty. The most pressing consideration is how to support students in identifying their purpose—in other words, what sits at the center of their affinities, strengths, and abilities to contribute to solving big, hairy, audacious challenges. This self-discovery and exploration process underlies all, and it's this common purpose that unites teachers and creates space for them to collaborate and support each other despite differences in the disciplines or industries they represent.

Students are not held captive inside the four walls of a traditional classroom; rather, they are deployed in teams to solve problems. In contrast to a more traditional career and technical education (CTE) program, the CAPS model enables students to be professional associates, working as consultants to the businesses and nonprofits in their community.

This process of profession-based learning is distinct from both problem-based learning and project-based learning in the levels of authenticity and depth. Table 7.1, below, shows some of the distinctions. It positions the student as the go-to contact for the client and enables the development of professional skills. When students serve as consultants, they feel the just-in-time energy of a real-world project. They realize something: This is not a simulation! This is not an assignment for a grade that will eventually land in a trash can! A real client is depending on them!

For example, CAPS engineering students worked with one mentor to create a solution for the mentor's autistic son, Joshua. The problem? Joshua was about to enter school, and he sometimes needed a fair amount of sensory pressure on his body in order to calm down and concentrate. His father was worried about how he would fare in a traditional classroom for seven hours a day.

The CAPS students got to work prototyping a concept first known as the Hug Chair. Utilizing existing pump technology and rudimentary building skills, they constructed a piece of furniture that soothed him. The project ramped up in intensity as the students and mentor sensed this could be the prototype for a commercial product. Suddenly the engineering students were pulling in business students ("We need market research. How much would a therapist or parent pay for this?"), medicine students ("What else do we need to know about autism as we finalize the

TABLE 7.1 *Characteristics and elements of profession-based learning*

	Problem-based	Project-based	Profession-based
Time frame	Short, within one to two class periods	Longer, will require several class periods over several weeks	Longer, will require working in and out of class over several weeks
Relationship	Student and teacher	Student and teacher	Student and client
Number of participants	Individual effort, typically not a team activity	Individual or team effort	Team effort, groups of three students is optimal
Curriculum type	"Off the shelf," not usually customized	"Off the shelf" or customized	Organized by the client
Skill type	Single technical skill; lower range of Bloom's Taxonomy	Multiple technical and soft skills; middle range of Bloom's Taxonomy	Multiple technical and soft skills; high range of Bloom's Taxonomy with emphasis on critical thinking
Focus	Developed from lecture content	Can be on a simulated real-world problem	Real problem(s) with solutions that could be implemented by the client
Method of assignment	"Turn in" work	"Turn in" work	Differentiated, promote options for students to choose
Method of assessment	No rubric; objective evaluation with emphasis on public presentation of recommendation	Rubric-based subjective evaluation	Differentiated, subjective evaluation
Example	A lease/buy problem requiring the use of Excel	Alleviating poverty in the local community	Developing a social media strategy for a new nonprofit organization

design?"), and education students ("How do we build a chair that will fit appropriately in a classroom and not be a distraction?"). Eventually, the Sensory Chair emerged as a final product, received an Edison Award (the first time students had ever won one of these prestigious prizes), and was acquired and licensed internationally.[1]

It is important to emphasize that CAPS is for students of any background and on any trajectory. Historically, CTE courses have been marketed to students not planning to attend a postsecondary institution. Unfortunately, you can still find examples of schools directing students toward CTE because educators don't think those students can perform at the same level as academic-track kids. This results in de facto segregation based on perceived ability level, with the "smarter" students gravitating toward college prep and the "not as smart" students corralled into CTE courses. In contrast, CAPS provides a meeting place for the worlds of college prep and career-ready programming. The vast majority of CAPS students attend a postsecondary institution after graduating high school.

CREATING THE CAPS NETWORK

In a previous life, I spent nearly two decades in the worlds of entrepreneurship and economic development. And I loved my work—so much so that I nearly laughed a friend of mine out of the room when she suggested I consider a job opportunity at a local school district. Out of courtesy, I pledged to review whatever information she sent to me, knowing full well that it would not change anything. Until it did. The thought of working with young people—igniting and harnessing their energy around a passion and purpose—was magical. Sure enough, in 2014, I became the newly minted executive director of Blue Valley CAPS.

When we are in a context that is far from our usual one, it's easier to see what would otherwise be invisible. It's one of the reasons I am writing this chapter from the heart of Finland. My senses are on fire here. Nothing is normal, so there is no autopilot. When I joined Blue Valley CAPS, as confusing and disorienting as the experience was for me, the ability to see the new world I entered through an outsider's perspective was a great gift. I was able to observe and interpret the system uninhibited by familiarity with the status quo.

One of the things I noticed immediately was that the program was driving student engagement through the roof, and people were taking note. School districts and community leaders from around the world came to tour the program. They witnessed high school students falling over each other to share with complete strangers the projects they were working on, the clients they supported, and what their experience was telling them about their future. The CAPS facility had a palpable energy to it. When we asked our guests to explain what they were experiencing, the best answer we ever got was: "This place is magical!"

Coming from the entrepreneurial world, I spotted a scalable opportunity and wanted to determine what we could do to catalyze relationships with those who were intrigued by the program and wanted to provide their own students with similar experiences.

Thus CAPS Network, a consortium of innovative school districts offering students profession-based learning, was born. From an inaugural set of fourteen affiliate programs in 2015, membership grew steadily, pushing over fifty programs by 2018. The model was growing not only in number of members but also geographic diversity. Spanning a number of states domestically, the addition of the American School of Bombay in Mumbai, India, gave CAPS international legs.

To manage the growth and seek new opportunities for scale, the Blue Valley School District authorized the creation of a nonprofit organization, CAPS Network, Inc., in 2020, with a formal 501(c)(3) designation provided by the IRS in April 2021.

We now have more than one hundred CAPS affiliate programs and 180 school districts across twenty-three states and four countries. The CAPS Network currently serves fourteen thousand high school students annually.

RESULTS THAT MATTER

The early 2000s ushered in an intense focus on standardized testing, born out of a desire to drive all students to mastery of content across traditional subjects like math and language arts. For decades, school districts have used test scores and traditional zero to one hundred grading scales as the measuring stick for success. As a result, lifelong educators have been hesitant to fully embrace models like profession-based learning, in part because of the disconnect between what we believe success looks like for CAPS students and more traditional measures.

Models like CAPS's profession-based learning recognize that students who build durable skills are more adaptable to, and competitive in, several industry lanes. At CAPS Network, we don't measure success based on testing. Instead, we survey students and measure their growth in confidence in skills that employers seek. In a recent survey of around two thousand students, reflecting on their experience to date, the proportion of students reporting confidence in the following professional skills jumped dramatically:

- Professional communication: 14 percent to 82 percent
- Building a professional resume: 13 percent to 74 percent
- Delivering an effective elevator pitch: 13 percent to 67 percent
- Professional presentation: 23 percent to 77 percent
- Professional conversations: 25 percent to 81 percent
- Accessing a professional network: 12 percent to 66 percent
- Owning strengths and passion: 27 percent to 78 percent
- Collaborating on a team: 38 percent to 84 percent
- Planning and executing a project: 23 percent to 77 percent
- Positively responding to a mistake: 32 percent to 80 percent
- Ability to be successful: 36 percent to 83 percent
- Level of career awareness: 15 percent to 83 percent[2]

As students graduate from high school and enter postsecondary institutions and the workforce, the positive trendlines continue. The 2023 CAPS Network Alumni Impact Report contains additional cause for optimism.[3] With over one thousand alumni participating, this report shows the program had a significant impact on students' professional growth and development. The findings indicate that CAPS alumni are lifelong learners, with a considerable percentage pursuing higher education. Alumni reported that CAPS had a substantial influence on their education and career decisions, with over three-fourths rating the impact as seven or higher on a scale of zero to ten. The study also showcases the tangible impact of CAPS in equipping students with skills that are crucial to their professional journeys. Rated on a scale from zero to five, CAPS alumni rated skills such as the ability to positively respond to mistakes, overall confidence in oneself, and conducting a one-on-one conversation with a professional at an average of 4.8.

Beyond the quantitative data, a former CAPS student recently reflected: "CAPS changed my life in unimaginable ways. I am forever thankful." Another was more specific about the direction the experience provided:

> As a senior I was a bit burnt out of the traditional classroom experience but was also unsure of the career path I wanted in the healthcare field. CAPS provided me an escape from the traditional classroom and allowed me to explore virtually every facet of the healthcare field and put me in the room with people I previously only dreamed of having the chance to talk to.

LIVING BRIDGES

While the impact CAPS Network has had is exciting, it is just the beginning of the real challenge—working together to improve the lives of students. These relationships include those among students, between students and professionals, between educators and professionals, and among educators. This work is about building the connective tissue between these nodes of our network.

Peter Diamandis is the founder of the XPRIZE, a series of open competitions intended to inspire and empower humanity to achieve breakthroughs that accelerate an abundant and equitable future for all. He uses two concepts to explain the power of a network. *Massively transformative purpose* (MTP) is a clear statement that guides, empowers, and inspires a network; it helps a network decide what to do and, more importantly, what not to do. A *living bridge* is a connection between people within a network that generates real emotions—because people join networks for the ideas, but they stay for the emotions. In other words, a meaningful MTP has the power to identify those who share your purpose. When you are able to identify your collaborators, you can create powerful and sustaining connections through living bridges.

In the CAPS Network, we defined our MTP as *always going where students lead*. Fully leaning into this mission has inspired an incredible dynamism. The CAPS framework is organized around five core values—profession-based learning, professional skills development, self-discovery and exploration, entrepreneurial mindset, and responsiveness—and we refer to these values as *the glue that holds us together.* The values provide guardrails and guidance for our affiliates to activate a new approach where students order their learning around their passions and purpose. For example, Little Rock Public Schools leveraged the CAPS MTP to redefine career and technical education for their students and teachers. Through the launch of Little Rock Excel, the district kick-started profession-based learning with deeper engagements directly with industry professionals in the community. With initial success in fields like medicine, engineering, and technology, the district is now using the CAPS framework to provide more students with opportunities to direct their own learning across all career pathways.

Once we clearly established the MTP, CAPS Network prioritized the curation of relationships among key stakeholders within the affiliate programs. We established regular opportunities for program directors to collaborate in real time, and we emphasized that they should get to know each other personally and professionally and discuss the similarities and differences between their approaches. Video calls, in tandem with asynchronous connections through the CAPS tech platform, allow members to share best practices, troubleshoot current challenges, and celebrate successes. All are powerful ways to build and grow living bridges, accelerating the work network-wide.

Through the years, members have established relationships that go beyond that of the typical colleague. In fact, affiliated educators have been known to describe opportunities to see fellow CAPS professionals as family reunions. We have intentionally nurtured these relationships to build trust and empathy among CAPS members through shared opportunities and challenges. Our ability to create something so special comes from educators' desires to connect with others who share their MTP and a dogged determination by our staff to invest time and resources into making these connections via living bridges.

PROGRESS TOWARD SCALE

The work of accelerating the impact of CAPS has been a blessing. Yet we are nowhere near making K–12 systems change a reality. Not even close.

In the United States, there are over thirteen thousand public school districts and thousands of private schools collectively serving over seventy-five million students. Each district has several individuals who have authority to make important decisions about staff and students. Each district also has several board members who can set the strategic direction of that district. In addition, each state operates differently, setting standards, rules, and priorities that vary. If you factor in just superintendents, school board members, and state division and agency heads, there are well over one hundred thousand decision-makers setting our course. It can hardly be surprising that one of the biggest challenges facing innovators in the education sector is the fragmentation of the market.

How do we significantly change and improve this system when the market is this fragmented? How do we accelerate pockets of positive change into more systems-level reforms?

Three realities are important to digest if we wish to accelerate innovation and systems change:

Top-down change does not work. Top-down approaches to tweaking the K–12 education system are rigid and do not account for the diverse needs of individual schools and communities. As a result, educators often notoriously resist change—particularly when they have little say in the matter. Can you blame them? When left out of the decision-making process, an educator's motivation to implement change with fidelity fades. In the end, the result is a lack of efficiency due to slow local engagement. This counteracts any efficiency gained by using top-down authority to launch the reform effort.

Bottom-up change is not exponentially scalable. There are many benefits that come from grassroots energy and locally driven, unencumbered innovation. One of the most exciting elements of entrepreneurship is the spirit of competition, which drives product creation and refinement. Unfortunately, locally generated innovations are often inherently isolated and do not scale. This is a problem if we truly desire to flip the K–12 system from an industrial, top-down, content-is-king behemoth to one that values context alongside content knowledge, adaptability over academia, and discovery of purpose over compliance to authority. In our work this past decade surveying innovative school models across the country, one thing is abundantly clear: there is no shortage of innovation in K–12; rather, the shortage is transferable innovation that is capable of impacting the millions of learners waiting to feel inspired.

There is potential for success using a network-of-networks framework. We've seen this in an experiment conducted by Northeastern University. The Boston-based college experimented with an alternative approach to scale: the concept of building a network of networks. A term ripped from the world of technology, a network of networks provides associations, affinity groups, or other networks a collaborative sandbox for discussion and experimentation that isn't contained to just one sphere. Most famous for its renowned cooperative education program—an opportunity for students to engage in experiential learning by allowing them to alternate between academic semesters and professional placements for real-world work experiences—Northeastern recognized the importance of aligning with like-minded organizations working toward a revolution in education. The initiative, titled the Network for Experiential Teaching and Learning (NExT), ultimately ran out of steam after a worthy attempt involving very capable and motivated people. (CAPS Network and Northeastern worked together in a formal strategic partnership for three years in an attempt to propel the effort.)

Despite the challenges faced by NExT, the network of networks strategy still has potential to foster and advance a movement that can attract the many purpose-driven stakeholders operating in the K–12 system. That said, we must be mindful of the challenges of activation.

The network of networks approach is not perfect, but it may still be the best approach to achieve the scale sought by those who prioritize top-down change and the local buy-in and contextual relevance desired by those who prioritize change from the bottom up. It recognizes the need for many different approaches to achieving change at scale, maintains some healthy competition and commensurate opportunities to learn from others, and sets the stage for elevating a long-term commitment to shared purpose alongside the short-term goals for individual entities' success and impact.

ADOPTING A MOVEMENT MENTALITY

A network of networks can produce real change and, in turn, unleash a movement. Movements have built-in energy. You can feel a movement. It is not a curriculum, product, or program. It has a life of its own and is not confined to anyone's rules, like the power of Mother Earth that my family witnessed in Yellowstone National Park: the spewing of water in the form of majestic geysers, the gurgling of mud pots, and the whistling of steam pockets—actions that are powerful and unconfined, yet serve an important purpose (geological pressure release).

It's also important to recognize that leadership of a movement is a responsibility for the many, not authority for the few. The greatest movements in history have involved ordinary people engaging in extraordinary ways that inspired collective action: Rosa Parks refusing to give up her seat on a Montgomery bus; Harriet Tubman working the Underground Railroad; and, more recently, Greta Thunberg leveraging the power of social media to spur action to combat climate change. It is important to note that neither Rosa, Harriet, nor Greta had any level of systematic authority when they started their work.

Relatedly, a longtime friend and ally recently asked me what it would look like to create a movement around the purpose CAPS serves. I was quick to interject that, while I strongly believe you can support and even steer a movement, you cannot create one. A prominent example from modern history is the #MeToo movement. While the movement had started in 2006, when Tarana Burke first began commenting on her own experiences, it picked up steam in 2017 when thousands of sexual abuse victims stepped forward in a matter of hours to share their stories. These people, mostly women, were motivated and empowered through shared experience, not by any one individual's agenda or authority. Movements thrive on authentic, human-to-human connections that create empathic cultures and foster a sense of belonging that is essential for next-level thinking and doing.

Finally, a challenge that has caused many movements to lose traction is that movements require selflessness and a willingness to serve purpose first. The goal of a movement—to make significant progress on a big adaptive challenge—differs from the goals of individual for-profits, nonprofits, or school districts. Organizations operating to meet their own missions are typically metric-driven and attentive to brand strength and promotion. In the short term, this approach is business-savvy. But the long-term consequence is a missed opportunity to cultivate a deeper level of impact. In other words, an intense focus on the broader purpose of your work will require you to reach a new level of selflessness.

How do more of us generate a movement mentality to change the face of education as we know it? What can we do to lean into the purpose we share to make real, significant impact, ultimately tipping the system of K–12 education toward one that is more active, relevant, authentic, and engaging for students?

I posit a few suggestions to get us started:

Identify the people who share your purpose. Before you take any action, it is important to pause and identify the individuals in your ecosystem who are doing similar (but not the same) work with a shared purpose. Part of the power in a movement comes from partnering with people who are striving to meet the same ultimate goal, even if they get there through different approaches. In fact, we learn more when our partners are diverse.

Within the CAPS Network, the variety of approaches taken by local programs to meet our core values is what generates the most spinoff innovation and experimentation. For example, an instructor of the original CAPS Global Business course in Blue Valley adjusted her approach to scheduling client-connected projects after hearing about a differing structure operated by a fellow CAPS instructor in Bentonville, Arkansas. The previous approach of diving deep into a semester-long consulting project with one corporate partner shifted to several rapidly cycled projects across many business verticals, such as marketing, finance, data analytics, and others. This change is now fostering student self-discovery and a healthy team competition dynamic that is driving more robust solutions for industry partners in the Kansas City area.

Care enough to be curious. Identifying people who share your purpose is a good start, but ultimately it's not sufficient if we want to truly alter

K–12 education. We also must care enough to be curious. To this end, we should ask the following questions:

- What could I learn from the people I've identified?
- What are they doing in their model that we are not?
- Why are they doing the work the way they are?
- Are there elements of their approach we should consider incorporating into our organization to influence more districts, schools, and educators?

One example that helps me embrace curiosity is happening as I write this chapter. The National Academy Foundation (NAF) is a national education nonprofit that supports high schools in the implementation of robust career academies. With a particular emphasis on addressing economic and social disparities, NAF has been bringing together schools and businesses around career prep for more than forty years. While it would be easy to see NAF as a competitor to CAPS Network, I have been asking the questions above and actively seeking opportunities to work with NAF to collectively scale our impact around our shared purpose. This has been surprisingly useful and has included insights about how to structure corporate partnerships and gather data. In the midst of remaining in a state of curiosity, we've begun exploring how to support each other's efforts in the name of giving more students exceptional, authentic learning.

We need to model curiosity for our students. We cannot ask them to do something we are not willing to do ourselves. We are all better off living with curiosity.

Intentionally ask, "How can I help you?" How often do we get so engrossed in our own world that we shift into "What can you do for me?" mode instead of pausing and asking others, "How can I help you?" A friend of mine, Alana Muller, has built a business around the fact that people are generally terrible at this. Her philosophy, which is embodied in her business—appropriately titled Coffee Lunch Coffee—is that networking is more than a way to get your immediate needs met. Rather, networking should be seen as a way to authentically engage other human beings, seeking to understand where purpose may be shared and how you can present yourself as a giver, not a taker.

I can say from experience that often, without even knowing it, we slip into a mentality that is hyperfocused on maximizing short-term value for our organizations. It's easy to fall into this trap when you serve a cause and truly believe in your work. After all, the more good we can do, the better the world will be, right? The truth is that we need each other more than ever, regardless of what cause or brand you represent. "How can I help?" can unlock new pathways for impact. You just have to be patient and be willing to go there.

In the early years of elevating our nonprofit, I found myself approaching conversations seeking wins for CAPS. Specifically, I recall being far too focused in my attempts to extract as much value as possible from every conversation. While in the moment it seemed the most direct route to success, on reflection I completely missed the chance to support others striving to achieve the same goals as I was.

Follow up, cheerlead . . . and mean it! In a world moving so rapidly, it is easy to take steps one through three and feel good about yourself but then drop the ball on follow-up. The reason it's so difficult to follow up is that doing so can appear to others as a waste of time—or, worse, a concession to your competitors. Do I take precious time to learn more and start brainstorming ways to support other organizations' efforts? Is my board of directors going to understand why I'm potentially helping my direct competitors? Despite these perceived barriers, it's important to follow up because doing so helps spur the movement along. Once you make a meaningful connection, don't be shy about cheerleading those who share your purpose. It's incredibly powerful for others to see you promoting competitors. This is a signal that you're trying to unleash a movement that extends beyond your bottom line.

Just recently, we have used our platforms at CAPS Network to cheerlead other brands in our ecosystem, particularly those that provide services that are tangential to ours. Examples include Open Way Learning, District C, and Learner-Centered Collaborative—all organizations that serve similar (if not the same) customers, yet add incredible value beyond our organization's capacity. Each of these organizations is driving the change we see as necessary to flip the K–12 system.

Partner beyond your brand and see what happens. I have a friend, Rich Sheridan, who cofounded a rather unusual software company, Menlo Innovations. Menlo is renowned for its culture, which is characterized by an open and collaborative workspace and by an explicit focus on joy in the workplace. Rich never says "no" to any of his employees' ideas or suggestions. He simply replies with three words: "Run the experiment." This approach drives up engagement in their workplace and unearths previously unseen opportunities.

Schools and education intermediary organizations must work up the courage to experiment, and one important way to do so is by partnering beyond brand. This could take any number of forms, but the consistent idea is that no single brand is best positioned to solve every problem with the best solution. In the case of our work at CAPS Network, I will share what I tell our own team on a weekly basis: if we care about the shared purpose of getting every student an authentic learning experience aligned with their interests, we should not care who provides the experience. Purpose should always trump brand. To that end, we have referred schools to other networks (our "competition") and steered clear of forcing partnerships for the sake of growing our membership. We stand by our greater purpose.

FIN FROM FINLAND

As I wrap up at my new favorite coffeehouse in Helsinki, I am thankful that we live in a world of possibilities, where seemingly anything is possible if we have the vision and the will. We will need both of these virtues in order to unleash a movement in K–12 education that radically changes the student experience for the better.

We can do this. It will just take us plowing our energy into creating deep and meaningful connections, the willingness to join a movement that we can help lead but cannot control, and a commitment to shared purpose over our individual goals and interests.

8

The Future of Math

Joel Rose

Welcome to sixth-grade math, Adrian. I'll be one of your teachers, Ms. Callahan.

Did you know there are approximately three hundred math skills you need to learn, understand, and apply to be ready for high school and beyond? I checked and it looks like you are entering sixth grade already knowing sixty of those skills, which means our goal is to help you learn around eighty new ones each year for the next three years. That may sound like a lot, but it's only about two to three per week—a very doable pace.

Our goal at Looscan Middle School is to help you learn all these skills and to be with you every step of the way. You'll learn some of these skills with me, some with other teachers, some with your class-mates, some with your family, and some by yourself. You'll get to learn them at school, at the local community center, and at home. You can even get ahead by learning more during the summer if you'd like to. All along the way, you'll also work on projects that help you apply these math skills in the real world so you can see the beauty and complexity of math.

We want to meet you where you are, give you a path to get to where you need to be, and help you learn to love math along the way. Let's get to work!

A DIRTY LITTLE SECRET

I was about to start my first year as a teacher when I asked my principal what I feared was a dumb question. The performance data for my incoming fifth-grade class showed some students were performing at a second-grade level, some at an eighth-grade level, and the rest everywhere in between. My job was to use the fifth-grade textbooks to teach the fifth-grade standards, which would ultimately be assessed on the fifth-grade end-of-year test.

I asked him how I was supposed to reconcile these two realities, and that's when he let me in on education's dirty little secret:

"Just do your best, Mr. Rose. That's what we all do."

Thirty years later, the reality hasn't changed much. Just before the pandemic, the average fifth-grade classroom had students performing at seven different grade levels.[1] That gap has since only widened.[2]

Nonetheless, policymakers, systems leaders, and advocates continue to assume that our nation's math woes can be solved by promoting a series of policies and reforms aimed at just about everything *except* how a teacher is supposed to differentiate instruction: raise standards, improve curricula, address teacher quality, adopt new assessments, instill accountability, lower class size, and increase teacher pay.

While each of these initiatives has been an important step forward for the sector, it's hard to say that any one of them (much less all of them) has resulted in a material difference in student outcomes. In 2005, 30 percent of eighth-grade students in the United States were proficient in math on the National Assessment of Educational Progress (NAEP). That number grew to 35 percent in 2011 but has since declined to 26 percent as of 2022.[3]

Proponents of these reforms will often point to progress on different tests, with different grade spans, and at different periods of time. But squinting to find signs of progress masks the larger truth: even with the incremental changes these tests sometimes reflect, it would still take at least another century before the vast majority of students leave high school with math skills that would allow them to succeed in college or a career.

If math outcomes are ever going to meaningfully improve, something more fundamental must change—something that can make it possible to differentiate teaching.

THE ONE MODALITY ASSUMPTION

In the United States, the idea of putting twenty-eight or so students into an eight-hundred-square-foot room with a teacher and a textbook dates back to the nineteenth century, when Horace Mann set up the nation's first set of compulsory schools in Massachusetts. Mann had a vision for what public schools should look like and how they should be organized. His writings included detailed specifications on everything from how students would be grouped to what subjects would be taught, where the desks were placed, and where the clock would hang.

Mann's classroom model was based on the assumption that there was one way for students to learn in school: from a teacher. Since teachers could teach only one skill at a time, and since schools needed to be organized around a fixed number of teachers, setting up schools to work like teacher-filled factories—where all same-age students followed the same curriculum—was perhaps the only sensible way for schools to be organized in the nineteenth century.

The limitations of Mann's approach to schooling may have been apparent to some, but there weren't any viable alternatives. States were adopting compulsory education laws and needed a plan for building and running schools. There were also some education leaders who believed the limitations of Mann's vision were a feature, not a bug. Among the most prominent was E. L. Thorndike, the nation's first educational psychologist, who published many of the textbooks and tests those schools used. Thorndike was a noted sexist, antisemite, and believer in eugenics who recognized the limitations of the delivery model but thought it would help to winnow out those he thought less worthy or capable.[4]

The Implications for Math

The consequences of a one-size-fits-all classroom model vary by age and subject. In early elementary reading, the consequences of not mastering phonics can be devastating for students' future success.[5] But assuming students can decode, they are generally able to engage in the basics of science and social studies even if they don't grasp all of the specifics taught in elementary school. In those subjects, themes are broad, content repeats, and the topics are not as cumulative.

But in math, where so many of the specific skills students learn in one year are essential to what they learn the next year, the implications of organizing instruction around their age, as opposed to what they already know, are profound.

From the time a child understands basic numeracy, there are approximately three hundred distinct math skills to learn in order to be ready for college, career, or the military. These skills include everything from finding the perimeter of a rectangle and calculating percentages from ratios to solving multistep equations. Mastering these skills requires understanding the procedures and concepts, as well as being able to apply them in combination and in real-world contexts.

States embed these skills within the language of their learning standards, and while there is some variation across states in how the standards are described and structured, most agree on what needs to be learned. States also organize these standards by grade level in ways that recognize the cumulative nature of math. For example, students learn how to multiply decimals in fifth grade, which prepares them to understand percentages in sixth grade, which is foundational to their applying percentages in seventh grade.

Table 8.1 shows New Classrooms' analysis of the number of on-grade skills and the foundational pre-grade skills that attach to each grade level, assuming students have already developed basic numeracy skills.[6] (Note that not every skill covered in one school year is foundational to the skills taught in the next year. Some skills are important but not foundational to any additional skills, while others may be foundational to skills taught two or three years later.)

Our nation's approach to teaching math is to organize instruction around only the on-grade skills *regardless of students' incoming foundational knowledge.* A fourth-grade teacher teaches the forty-two fourth-

TABLE 8.1 *Number of distinct math skills learned in fourth grade through Algebra 1*

Grade level	Number of on-grade skills	Number of foundational pre-grade skills	Total on-grade and foundational pre-grade skills
4	42	22	64
5	40	49	89
6	46	73	119
7	42	80	132
8	49	89	138
Algebra 1	52	95	147

Note: While some students take Algebra 1 in eighth grade (or even seventh grade) based on academic readiness and/or course availability, most take Algebra 1 in ninth grade or later.

grade skills, the fifth-grade teacher teaches the forty fifth-grade skills, and so forth.

It's an approach that only works if students never fall behind.

But students *do* fall behind for any number of reasons: quality of instruction, learning differences, student mobility, personal trauma, student illness, teacher illness, absenteeism, a pandemic, and more. And as students are promoted from one grade to the next—despite not mastering the required math skills—many fall even further behind.

This is likely a key reason why, between 2018 and 2022, math scores in the United States on the Programme for International Student Assessment dropped thirteen points while reading scores remained flat. It may also be why drops in math scores were far more acute than those in reading on the most recent round of NAEP.[7]

Math education rests on the assumptions that instruction needs to be conducted solely by the teacher and that teaching should focus on the skills reflected in the student's enrolled grade level. So long as those assumptions prevail, it's hard to see how math achievement will ever materially improve.

MODALITIES CHANGE THE GAME

In the early 2000s, as the internet was reshaping nearly every sector in our economy, a friend suggested we meet at his office before venturing off to lunch. I'd been working for a school management company, and he'd been running an adult learning center, training a generation of would-be technicians and programmers on the skills they needed to land a new job. As I sat waiting for him to come out, I saw a sign hanging in the waiting room that I couldn't stop staring at:

"Choose Your Modality: Live, Online, or Blended."

My friend explained that a modality was simply a way of delivering instruction on a particular concept. All students within a course followed a standard curriculum, but the center scheduled in-person instruction on different modules at different times. It also provided students with asynchronous instruction on each of the modules, allowing them to learn everything at home or to come in periodically to engage more directly with the teacher. Common assessments helped to measure progress along the way.

I thought about Rolando, a former student of mine, and how lost he looked when I was teaching my students how to multiply decimals because he didn't yet understand what a decimal was. Would those precious instructional hours have been better spent teaching him about decimals, even if it were through a modality that wasn't me?

On the other end was Eliana. She began the year well beyond grade level and was easily able to master what I was teaching. Should she have been learning something far more advanced, even if I wasn't teaching it to her?

For both of them, even if the other modalities might not have been as good as what I could have done as a teacher, any loss in instructional quality might have been offset by the fact that each student would have been working on the right skill at the right time.

Richard Elmore, the late professor of education at Harvard best known for his work on the instructional core, said there were only three ways to improve student learning at scale:

- Increase the teacher's instructional knowledge and skill (capacity).
- Increase the level of complexity of the content students must learn.
- Change the role of the student in the instructional process.[8]

That all may be true—but it assumes schools continue to operate within the original classroom model that Mann envisioned.

Perhaps the introduction of modalities beyond teacher-led, whole-class instruction meant that it was time to revisit the instructional core itself.

IF YOU BUILD IT

After visiting the adult learning center, I began to wonder what a multi-modal math classroom would look like, so I drafted a proposal for how it might work. I called it School of One and shared the draft with Joel Klein, then the New York City Public Schools chancellor, for whom I was working at the time. He took to the idea and helped raise the initial funding to get it off the ground.

Here is how it worked:

At the beginning of the school year, each participating student took a diagnostic assessment that generated a personalized set of skills (including procedural, conceptual, and applied understanding) to work on over the course of the school year. That list could include a combination of pre-grade, on-grade, and post-grade skills, depending on where each student was starting.

When it was time for math, students would enter the math center (often several combined classrooms set up with multiple learning stations) and view an airport-like television monitor that displayed their name and which station they should report to. The stations were designed to support different modalities, including teacher-led instruction, collaborative learning, real-world tasks, and independent learning.

Each day, students would focus on a specific skill, experienced via two different modalities, before taking an online "exit slip" assessment and then transitioning to their next subject. The data from the exit slip fed a sophisticated scheduling engine, which in turn generated recommended plans and student groupings for the next day based on what each student now understood.

It was a hit. *Time* named School of One a "Best Invention of 2009," and with the support of several national funders, we later spun the idea out of the New York City Department of Education into a new nonprofit (New Classrooms) and renamed the program Teach to One so we could begin to expand to other schools and districts across the country.[9]

Over the next eight years, the program expanded to serve more than one hundred schools across twenty states. National and local press wrote extensively about the program, and hundreds of visitors from all around the world came to see it in action. Most importantly, a third-party study showed students learned 23 percent more than the national average and 53 percent more in schools where the conditions allowed for higher levels of implementation fidelity.[10]

But while many systems leaders and advocates found the model fascinating, schools weren't partnering with us as fast as we had initially hoped. District administrators had other priorities: the adoption of new standards, assessments, curricula, and teacher training.

There were also practical limitations that stood in the way of adoption. Implementing Teach to One initially required knocking down walls (we eventually figured out a single-classroom version), retraining teachers to teach collaboratively and across multiple grade levels, paying several times more than what a textbook costs, and challenging the wisdom of accountability systems that incentivized teaching only the grade-level standards. As one superintendent shared, "Teach to One has to be the future of math. But we just aren't ready for it. It's too big of a leap from where we are now."

He was right. And when the pandemic hit, the challenge of adoption and implementation became even more acute. Schools were focused on teaching via Zoom and in no mood to consider a radically new approach to math (much less one that could spur a superspreader event).

So, in 2020, we took what we learned from our initial model and launched Teach to One Roadmaps, an all-digital, asynchronous version that supplements a school's core curriculum. In just two years, it became more widely adopted than Teach to One.

Will Teach to One Roadmaps be as effective as our original model? While it does not yet have all the modalities, the scheduler, or the project-based tasks that were core parts of the initial Teach to One model, it does have one key advantage over the original version: it gives students and teachers the ability to better understand and manage learning pace.

UNLOCKING PACE

In April 2023, researchers at the Center for Research on Education Outcomes (CREDO) released their analysis of school and district efforts to catch students up from pandemic-related learning losses.[11] Schools spent billions of federal dollars on new grade-level curricula, training teachers, hiring tutors, and providing summer and afterschool programs. But according to the researchers, it was largely all for naught.

At the heart of the CREDO study was the question of learning pace. The researchers used state test data to understand how far behind students were performing and then determined that a return to the prepandemic pace of learning would simply not be enough for students to catch back up.

Our own skill-level analysis further reinforced this reality.

Students are *supposed* to learn an average of forty-five grade-level math skills each year beginning in fourth grade and going through Algebra 1. Assuming thirty instructional weeks (a typical thirty-six-week school year minus the time allocated for testing, field trips, fire drills, etc.), that means a student is *supposed* to learn an average of 1.5 new skills per week. That's possible, but only for the minority of students who never fall too far behind.

For those who do fall behind, achieving 1.5 skills per week isn't just improbable. It's also insufficient. In Teach to One Roadmaps partner schools, for example, the average student begins the school year knowing 30 percent of the combined pre-grade and on-grade skills required to achieve full proficiency at that grade level. This means that an incoming seventh-grade student, for example, would need to maintain a pace of 3.1 skills per week to achieve full proficiency. Older students with more years of accumulated gaps would have to learn even faster to achieve proficiency.[12]

Would a shift to personalized competency-based learning (PCBL) provide students with a better chance of accelerating by focusing instructional hours on the skills they are most ready to learn?

That's what the science of learning says. Among the most foundational principles of cognitive science is that students have limited working memory capacities, which can be overwhelmed by tasks that are too cognitively demanding.[13] As students memorize information and master skills, their brains are free to use their working memory on other, higher-order tasks. But if they don't master those lower-order skills, then their working memory strains to deal with both the simple and more complex tasks they are facing. As a result, understanding new ideas can be impeded if students are confronted with too much information at once.[14] (Imagine, for example, trying to solve two-step equations without an understanding of variables and one-step equations.) To answer the question "Is the student ready?" researchers say it's best to first consider whether "the student mastered the prerequisites."[15]

PCBL also aligns with what's known about the social, emotional, motivational, and cognitive building blocks of learning. When a student is taught skills far beyond what they are ready to learn, it's easy for them to think they just aren't capable of learning at that level. This can undermine self-efficacy and agency and inhibit development of a growth mindset, making it even harder to learn new skills in the future.[16] Success, however, can build confidence and motivation to fuel future learning.[17]

We've seen the power of meeting individual student needs in our own data. In the original Teach to One, each skill had between one and four predecessor skills. Among those skills with four predecessors, students had an 80 percent chance of learning a target skill when they mastered all four predecessors. But the fewer predecessors the student had acquired, the lower their success rate. If they knew none of the predecessor skills, they had only a 6 percent chance of learning the target skill.

Similar evidence is now also emerging in Roadmaps partner schools: acceleration increases as students become more academically prepared to learn new skills—especially as they get older. In the 2022–23 school year, when Roadmaps was used as a supplement to schools' core curriculum, students learned at an average pace of 1.4 skills per week. In the highest-performing school, students averaged 2.5 skills per week. Those totals don't include the skills students learn in their core program, meaning their full annual pace was likely far higher.

Other program studies also speak to the value of meeting individual student needs through PCBL. For example, a comprehensive study of Saga Education, which served as the basis for allocating billions of dollars to high-dosage tutoring, examined three potential reasons for the program's impressive results. In this study, personalization—not simply the mentoring or improved classroom management aspects of the program—was the key to delivering big gains in math.[18]

The pace many middle and high schools need to achieve to catch up to grade level from pandemic learning loss is simply impossible if the focus remains solely on grade-level instruction. But an academic strategy that incorporates PCBL gives students a real chance to catch up and get ahead.

TACKLING THE BARRIERS

What keeps more schools and districts from embracing PCBL? Standing in the way are a series of misconceptions about PCBL, as well as a set of practical challenges that require creative solutions to overcome.

Confronting Misconceptions

PCBL is remediation

"Meeting students where they are" echoes the language of justification for remedial education, where lower-performing students are shuffled into classes that focus on material from prior grade levels and, as a result, never actually catch up.

There is also ample evidence that remediation disproportionately affects students from marginalized communities who may never access grade-level material because their teachers simply don't expect enough of them.[19] Expectations matter, and it's true that students can't learn what they haven't been taught.

At the same time, it is mastery, not access, that drives social mobility. And for many students, a focus on access may actually undermine a focus on mastery because precious instructional hours are spent teaching content students are unlikely to master.

PCBL is oriented around a third approach: meet students where they are *and* provide them with a viable pathway to get to where they need to be.

Skills at the expense of abstract thinking

Another objection comes from educators who argue that a systemic, skills-based approach to math education is anathema to the abstract thinking and problem-solving that are at the heart of a quality math education. The critique hearkens back to the math wars of the 1990s, when debates raged about whether deeper levels of conceptual and applied understanding should be incorporated into math education. The new California math framework resurfaced this tension.[20]

A shift to PCBL does not imply a return to rote teaching. The fact that some students need to focus on pre-grade skills does not mean that those skills should be taught in ways devoid of any of the key elements of high-quality pedagogy. Nor does it suggest that conceptual and applied understanding should not be part of mastery. On the contrary, a shift to PCBL recognizes that *better* understanding of foundational concepts is a prerequisite for *deeper* levels of understanding. Supporting students to ensure they master foundational concepts *increases* the likelihood that they will develop the ability to think more deeply.

Risks of incoherence

Opponents fear that a math classroom organized around PCBL will be less instructionally coherent and thus less effective—especially if students are jumping around to different mathematical domains, or if they are using materials from a variety of sources that teach concepts in different ways.

Dismissing PCBL because of risks to coherence not only disregards the science of learning and the need for foundational understanding, but also mistakenly presumes that the only way of achieving instructional coherence is by strict adherence to a fixed pedagogical approach on a predetermined sequence of connected skills *applied to a whole class.* Thoughtfully designed PCBL programs can be both instructionally coherent and effective for each student.

If the only way to drive instructional coherence is with a cohort-based instructional program, then the gaps students are left with essentially assure an overall incoherent understanding of math—with significant implications for their futures.

Overcoming Practical Challenges

A shift in mindset

School board members, district and school administrators, teachers, and parents have all grown up in a world where math instruction was based on a student's enrolled grade. The century-old predominance of this notion has created a set of expectations, built over generations, that will not easily be dislodged. It's easier and more familiar to keep using a grade-level textbook, following a standard scope and sequence, and testing relative to grade-level standards. Because students, parents, and policymakers are so familiar with the status quo, they are likely to resist upending it.

Some teachers may also struggle with the transition to PCBL, especially if they hold on to the ideas that they should be the sole source of instruction, that they should initiate and design the full student experience, or that it's their job to cover every skill included in the grade-level standards. These mindsets are incompatible with an embrace of PCBL.

Shifting these mindsets ultimately depends on the vision and resolve of leaders. Beginning a shift to PCBL requires them to authentically engage with math teachers to learn more about the limitations of grade-level-only instruction and to develop a shared vision for what a transition to PCBL will require.

Grade-level-only assessments

Federal law requires each state to assess all students in grades 3 through 8 (and once in high school) in reading and math, report on how students performed on grade-level standards, and implement a statewide accountability system that incorporates those results. Until the law changes, the federal focus on grade-level assessments raises the stakes for school and district leaders looking to move away from an exclusive focus on teaching grade-level material for fear that near-term scores might go down.

One way we've learned to address this challenge is by demonstrating to schools how skill completion within Teach to One Roadmaps correlates to success on the state assessment. Specifically, if students master all the skills on their personalized academic roadmap (which includes both grade-level skills and their relevant pre-grade skills), it's a near certainty that they will succeed on the state assessment.[21] Having this type of validity helps to earn the trust of educators who come to see that if they focus on skill acquisition and pace, results on the state test will follow.

Time

Most middle and high schools have either a single block (forty-five to sixty minutes) or double block (eighty to ninety minutes) allocated for their core math instruction each day. And most schools are not yet looking to jettison their core math program in favor of comprehensive PCBL models like the original Teach to One, whether because of the current accountability system, their recent investments in high-quality curriculum, or a belief that switching models would simply be too much change.

For those with double blocks or separate intervention periods, PCBL tools like Teach to One Roadmaps are now being used during the last twenty to thirty minutes of a core instructional block. This allows schools to provide both grade-level curriculum and PCBL. Other schools have scheduled intervention periods or afterschool sessions for struggling students to address their fundamental gaps with PCBL.

Schools with a single math block and a commitment to a core math program need to be more creative if they want to explore PCBL. One way is by using PCBL tools to *inform* core instruction. Teach to One Roadmaps, for example, helps teachers understand the precise pre-grade gaps each student has in relation to the unit they are teaching in the core math block so teachers can then incorporate that information into both their lessons and homework assignments. They can also use Teach to One Roadmaps as an exit slip generator, assigning students to take skill-level assessments on the topics they cover in their core math program so the teachers can both access reliable information on skill-level mastery and assign personalized homework.

Unachievable pace targets

In some cases, achieving the pace targets required for students to catch up in a single year may be highly improbable *even with* a high-quality implementation of PCBL. For example, a sixth-grade student who knows only 20 percent of the on-grade and pre-grade skills would need to maintain a pace of 3.2 skills per week over thirty weeks in order to fully catch up to grade level in a single year.

To overcome this challenge, some schools and districts may choose not to focus that sixth-grade student's learning progression on catching up to sixth-grade standards in a single year, but instead focus on a multiyear plan that exclusively targets the pre- and on-grade skills relating to *eighth* grade. That may sound odd, but if a sixth-grade student needs more than one year to catch up to sixth-grade standards, they would then still be behind because, by then, they would be enrolled in a higher grade level.

Targeting a future grade level, as opposed to the current one, allows schools to align the catch-up year to the grade students will be enrolled in. This becomes possible because the school can then prioritize a more narrow set of skills to focus on: fourth-, fifth-, sixth-, or seventh-grade skills that directly relate to eighth-grade proficiency. (There are, for example, skills relating to statistics and probability that aren't foundational to eighth grade.) This strategy reduces the total number of skills that need to be mastered over a three-year period, resulting in a required pace of 1.5 skills per week for thirty weeks each year for three years. Once students have mastered them all, they could then focus on those skills that were deprioritized.[22]

These are the kinds of opportunities that open up when schools transition to PCBL.

CONCLUSION

Math is cumulative based on skills. Grade levels are sequential based on age. Those realities inherently conflict with one another, no matter how strong the teacher, how good the curriculum, or how stringent the accountability system.

Historically, the age-grade paradigm has always prevailed. It is ingrained within our schools' operating systems, our collective mindsets, and our nation's policies. Yet efforts to move past incremental gains and *meaningfully* improve math education within the age-grade paradigm have never failed to disappoint—because it can't be done.

The tools and capabilities to move beyond this paradigm are now in our grasp. Thoughtfully deployed, they can enable true differentiated learning, with multiple learning modalities unlocking the ability to differentiate learning pace in ways that far exceed what's possible within the bounds of what Horace Mann envisioned.

It won't happen quickly. Meeting students where they are requires meeting schools where they are, and that means beginning with interim steps like PCBL-focused supplemental programs that can begin to get administrators and teachers comfortable working in a new way.

But over time, systems leaders and teachers will come to see the power of PCBL. They'll begin to view grade-level standards as general benchmarks that help inform if a student is on track, as opposed to rigid requirements that determine what they should and should not be taught. Supplemental programs will turn into core programs, federal accountability systems will shift to create space for PCBL, and more solutions will come on the market.

That's when the future of math will become just math.

9

Rethinking Assessment

Arthur VanderVeen

On March 20, 2020, then-secretary of education Betsy DeVos waived federal standardized testing requirements. For the first time in over twenty-five years, there would be no statewide accountability testing. This was the short-term result of schools being closed and teachers, students, and families frantically adapting to remote learning. But it would also have long-term implications for states' abilities to navigate the unprecedented disruptions to American schooling.

As students gradually returned to school starting in the fall of 2020, conversations turned to whether standardized testing would resume in the spring of 2021. Fierce discussions ensued, and it became clear that the disruption of this once-in-a-century pandemic could indeed tip the scales toward eliminating annual state testing requirements. For the first time since the introduction of No Child Left Behind in 2001, policymakers, teachers, and parents dared to ask, "Could this be the death of statewide accountability assessments?"

But the US Department of Education announced in February 2021 that states would in fact have to administer their end-of-year—also known as summative—assessments. While the department did allow states to seek waivers for certain circumstances, only the District of Columbia's request to waive statewide assessments outright was approved, as almost 90 percent of DC students were still learning remotely.

As the (admittedly compromised and limited) 2021 state assessment data rolled in, the unprecedented learning loss became clear. Alongside the National Assessment of Educational Progress, they indicated that pandemic-induced disruptions to learning had erased two decades of learning gains.

State and district leaders recognized that they needed better visibility into which grades, subjects, and student groups had been impacted most severely. The information was essential to inform recovery efforts and responsibly direct the $190 billion in federal funds made available to accelerate learning recovery, enable access to technology, and address health and safety concerns. Nationwide, state accountability testing resumed in spring 2022, and today, states are once again using data to identify schools that need comprehensive or targeted support.

While states continue to comply with traditional federal accountability requirements, a significant movement is emerging among states and advocacy organizations that recognize a once-in-a-century opportunity to rethink accountability assessments. As a coalition of leading policy organizations noted at the beginning of the recovery, "The massive disruption to instruction fueled a new urgency to rethink the potential of assessments to drive better teaching and learning."[1] Now, more than twenty states are piloting modifications to their statewide programs that include through-year assessments to replace or supplement a single end-of-year test; performance tasks that measure a richer set of competencies, often reflected in a "portrait of a graduate"; portfolio assessments; and high school capstone projects.

The magnitude of learning loss and the growing need for accelerated learning have opened the door for new thinking. There is new conviction that, going forward, tests must not only *measure what students learn* but also *help them learn*.

My company, New Meridian, is working on the technical and practical challenges of just such a system and seeing promising results. I believe we are, in fact, on the verge of a new era that will redefine assessments such that they help inform instruction in addition to measuring learning for accountability purposes.

WHY Θ (THETA) IS SUCH A POWERFUL TOOL FOR DISTRICT ADMINISTRATORS—BUT NOT FOR TEACHERS

Standardized assessments were not designed to help students learn. Reflecting late nineteenth- and early twentieth-century scientific management principles, which were developed to increase the efficiency of factory production systems, intelligence and achievement tests proliferated in the early 1900s. These assessments were adopted by a growing cadre of professional school administrators in large urban districts who subscribed to the ethos of precision and efficiency.[2]

Large urban school districts and state education agencies established bureaus of research, often staffed by graduates of the major test-producing universities: the University of Iowa, Stanford University, and Columbia University's Teachers College. Their development of multiple-choice test items and new scoring technologies pioneered by IBM helped to scale new, "objective" measures of students' mastery of school subjects, providing system administrators with the data they needed to evaluate and manage schools.

Managing a system of schools requires comparability; to support this, twentieth-century large-scale test design and psychometrics reduced all the complexity of student learning to a simple variable: Θ (*theta*).

Theta is the measure of a student's proficiency in a domain (for the following example, sixth-grade math). Assessments determine a student's theta by administering a set of tasks (test questions) that reflect what sixth-grade students should know and be able to do as defined by a state's learning standards. These test questions sample lightly from across the grade 6 standards, including working with fractions; reasoning with ratios; solving algebraic equations; finding the area of two-dimensional geometric shapes; and calculating a statistical mean, median, and mode. Psychometricians order the test questions according to difficulty, and experts and educators determine how many of the test questions students should get correct to be considered proficient in sixth-grade math.

If there are fifty-four questions on an end-of-year summative test, the math experts and educators might agree that thirty correct answers represents proficiency. Here's where the need for comparability comes in: to simplify our comparisons among students (and schools), we don't differentiate between students who are strong in geometry and weak in algebra or vice versa. For purposes of comparability, we don't care if a student is good at fractions, two-digit multiplication, division, or calculating the area of two-dimensional geometric shapes. Theta squeezes a whole lot of information into a simple assessment of whether or not a student is proficient at sixth-grade math.

For district administrators, theta is an incredibly powerful tool because they can count how many students at School A are proficient and compare that number to how many are proficient at School B. Administrators can disaggregate which students are and are not proficient by race or ethnicity, socioeconomic status, English language proficiency, and special education status. They can use these data to assign a math specialist to spend two days a week at School A and three days at School B and identify which students to work with in each school.

Nationally, schools administer eighty million summative math and ELA assessments to determine a theta for forty million tested students. States and districts use these data to compare schools and hold them accountable for student learning outcomes.

The data needed to manage schools and school systems, however, are different from the data needed to inform instruction. Theta cannot inform the math specialists which parts of the sixth-grade curriculum they need to focus on. It cannot reliably tell them which students are struggling with which parts of the curriculum. That requires *retesting* students with more fine-grained, diagnostic, or formative assessments, so that teachers or math specialists can target instructional interventions to the real learning needs of individual students.

This inefficiency—caused by testing for theta and then retesting to inform instructional decisions—is bewildering. I would argue, in fact, that the failure to design assessments *for* learning has created widespread dissatisfaction with current assessment systems and the seemingly intractable disconnect between the kinds of assessments required by accountability policy advocates and the needs and concerns of families, students, and teachers. Under our current regime, schools respond to the pressure of summative assessments by spending months—if not the entire year—on a narrow set of "power standards" on the end-of-year test. Districts adopt interim assessments to reinforce the focus on discrete skills that are decontextualized from any coherent instructional plan. The compounding effect transforms an entire year of instruction into a lifeless drilling of skills without considering whether students might learn more with a coherent, research-based curriculum. It's no wonder families and students opt out of state testing as a desperate means of throwing a wrench into our finely calibrated but misguided assessment and accountability systems.

This problem is not new. In fact, the entire standards-based education movement going back to the 1990s was premised on the belief that aligning curriculum, instruction, and assessments to explicit learning standards would achieve greater overall coherence and efficiency in our educational practices. An influential National Research Council report published in 2001, at the height of enthusiasm for the standards movement, captured this seemingly self-evident truth: "Ideally, an assessment should measure what students are actually being taught, and what is actually being taught should parallel the curriculum one wants students to learn. If any of the functions is not well synchronized, it will disrupt the balance and skew the educational process."[3] Just months later, however, No Child Left Behind ushered in a juggernaut of federally mandated state testing focused entirely on assessment *of* learning for accountability purposes. Until we address this imbalance between assessment *for* learning and assessment *of* learning, we will continue to distort instructional practices and frustrate the aspirations of educators, students, and families.

DESIGNING A STUDENT-FIRST APPROACH TO ASSESSMENT FOR LEARNING

One wonders why this has been so hard to fix. One can imagine a rich curriculum with regular, short checks for understanding that inform instruction and afford the opportunity to deepen and extend student learning—all personalized to the needs of individual students. Over the course of the year, these embedded assessments aggregate into a cumulative measure of students' mastery of the grade-level standards—theta—that yields a reliable, comparable score for accountability purposes.

Such an approach would eliminate the inefficiency of double testing and achieve two different goals: reduce the disconnect between what is taught in the classroom and what is measured by the state, and minimize the stress of a high-stakes, one-shot, multiday test at the end of the year.

Sounds compelling, right? So why don't such systems already exist?

The truth is, we are getting closer to this vision. Several of the twenty states that are currently piloting next-generation assessments are focusing on learner-focused through-year designs that, to varying degrees, measure what is taught when it is taught throughout the year and aggregate those short test scores into a final summative measure. I believe this challenge defines the future of educational assessment, if for no other reason than it has captured the imagination of educators, administrators, families, researchers, test vendors, philanthropic funders, and policymakers who all want to get more instructionally useful information out of state tests.

As I reflect on these challenges from the perspective of what I do, which is to develop large-scale accountability assessments for states, I have identified three design principles that I believe can help resolve the tension between assessment for learning that elicits and measures students' learning and assessment of learning that is capable of producing theta. First, assessments for learning are closely aligned to an instructional plan for introducing, developing, applying, and extending new knowledge and skills. Second, they provide actionable feedback to inform instructional decisions. And finally, they reflect the current understanding that students learn by making meaning rather than by memorizing facts. We need to design for these principles and figure out how to derive scaled measures of theta from this more formative information.

Align What Is Tested to What Is Taught, as It's Taught

Designing assessments for learning to support students' learning development throughout the year is very different from designing an assessment of learning at the end of the year. To guide and scaffold students' learning development, teachers need information that is intimately tied to what students are working on so they can make decisions about how to intervene to further students' progress toward proficiency.

Aligning assessments directly to what is taught, when it's taught, at scale, is not easy—and it's certainly not practicable for a state assessment program that allows local districts to choose their own curriculum. But that's exactly the system we have today: no curriculum publisher holds more than 20 percent of the market, and a long tail of publishers serve well under 10 percent. This diversity of options makes it difficult to align assessments with specific curriculum programs. To address this difficulty, we recommend a standards-based approach, which we think is more practical. This entails ensuring that short, modular assessments are aligned to the standards *as the standards are taught in the local district through their chosen curriculum.* Many district testing platforms support this by offering banks of existing standards-aligned test items or enabling teachers to author their own. The guiding principle here is that assessment for learning needs to be closely aligned to what is taught when it's taught. Most commercial interim assessments don't do this. Designed to yield theta, they measure student mastery of all the standards for a grade level each time they are administered so that they can provide a growth measure. The result: valuable instructional time is wasted testing students on material they haven't yet had an opportunity to learn, feedback is not granular enough to inform instructional decisions, and students do poorly and get frustrated with their results.

At New Meridian, we are experimenting with standards-aligned *test-lets* that can be flexibly aligned to local districts' curricula. These testlets provide both formative feedback on student learning progressions and a comparable, reliable measure of students' overall proficiency and growth. We do this by first measuring and reporting students' developing mastery of the knowledge, skills, and abilities that build toward standards mastery, which helps teachers support students along their developmental pathway. We then convert those data to a scale that reports each student's theta. This flips on its head the traditional approach of most interim assessments, which design for theta and then try to derive instructionally relevant subscores; these have been notoriously unreliable, and they are too general to inform instruction. We are proving that it's possible to derive both formative and summative measures of student learning from the same assessment tasks and scores, thereby eliminating the inefficiencies of having to test separately for both.

Of course, testing what's taught when it's taught is only the beginning. Teachers need to use that information to inform instructional decisions. Research has shown that district use of interim assessments has little impact on student achievement outcomes unless teachers are able to use the results to adapt their instruction. Teachers face tremendous structural barriers to using those data to adapt instruction, including lack of confidence in using data to inform instruction, frustration at feeling compelled to keep up with the pacing guide as they race toward preparing students for the state test, and lack of experience with differentiating instruction for a class of twenty-four to thirty students. Studies have even shown that asking less-experienced teachers to use data to inform instruction can *lower* student achievement outcomes.[4] The one intervention related to data-informed instruction that has been shown to correlate significantly with positive student learning outcomes is ensuring teachers have the time and flexibility to adjust instruction based on the data, to intervene, and to reteach. This one factor is stronger even than teachers' confidence in using data to inform instruction. This suggests administrators should allow teachers some flexibility in adhering to the pacing guide, and they should trust both the teachers' judgment and the student testing data to inform decisions about when students need more time to revisit concepts with additional feedback and support.

Focus on Learning Progressions Before Standards Mastery

Assessments for learning should be not only aligned to the standards as they are taught but also sensitive to students' progress toward standards mastery. This is critical to providing actionable feedback to support teachers' instructional decisions. Summative and interim assessments directly test standards mastery—what students should be expected to do once they have mastered the standard. Assessments for learning elicit and analyze evidence of students' thinking *along the way* in order to guide the students' emerging understanding toward mastery. That requires designing tasks that elicit evidence of students' learning development toward standards mastery, not merely testing the standards. Our task designers work closely with teachers and learning development specialists in each content area to support research-based learning progressions, including identifying misconceptions that can hinder learning development.

Once you're committed to measuring learning progressions rather than standards, you have to account for the fact that learning progressions in ELA are very different from those in math.

Beginning in grade 3, state accountability assessments in ELA measure reading comprehension rather than the development of foundational reading skills (such as phonemic awareness, phonics, and word attack skills, all foundational to a phonics-based approach). Once students have transitioned from learning to read to reading to learn, they holistically apply a complex but limited set of interrelated skills to construct the meaning of texts. At a high level, these skills are reflected in the Common Core State Standards as understanding key ideas and details, applying an understanding of the author's craft, and integrating both background knowledge and ideas from across texts. As readers develop these skills, they can apply them to increasingly complex texts with increasing fluency.

Math, on the other hand, is a very different domain. The concepts and procedures students learn are much more discrete and sequentially dependent. Students learn numbers and operations starting with whole numbers before progressing to fractions. Understanding fractions is foundational to understanding ratios and proportional reasoning. Assessments of students' learning progression in math throughout the year, therefore, can test the mastery of discrete concepts and procedures as they're learned, so that teachers can intervene and ensure students have the foundation they need to master what comes next in the progression.

At New Meridian, we are developing through-year assessment scoring models that account for these differences: For math, we map dependencies among specific standards within a learning progression and weight performance on later standards that assume mastery on earlier standards;

we then aggregate these weighted scores. For ELA, we adjust final scores according to the complexity of texts and tasks that students are ultimately able to master.

Prioritize Meaning-Making Over Knowledge

Finally, assessments for learning should reflect the modern understanding that students learn through a process of making meaning rather than one of rote memorization.

It seems intuitive to characterize learning as a process of making meaning: Some experience (or lesson) confronts us with new information. We struggle to make sense of it at first; we research the topic to deepen our understanding; we scan our past experience and understanding; we apply that experience and understanding to incorporate the new information; we modify our prior understanding. We have learned.

This, however, was not the prevailing model of learning through the first half of the twentieth century. Behavioral psychologists, such as John B. Watson and B. F. Skinner, characterized learning as building a set of learned associations between external stimuli and behavioral responses. Organisms (such as rats) learn which responses to a given stimulus result in beneficial outcomes (as when stepping on a pedal produces a piece of cheese). Behaviorists explicitly rejected the study of internal mental processes in favor of behaviors that could be easily and reliably observed and measured, shaping educational assessment's more externally focused and objective approach to testing. Indeed, behaviorism had a lasting impact on classroom practice.

As the thinking went, learned associations—recall of facts, fluency with algorithms, and the like—could be efficiently reinforced through drill-and-practice exercises, which would prepare students for standardized multiple-choice tests. Students demonstrate how much they have learned by reciting more and more facts and fluently demonstrating mastery of procedures. Getting eight out of ten questions correct reflects more knowledge than getting seven out of ten does. Like the scale on a measuring cup, theta measures student learning as a quantity of knowledge, making it possible to reliably compare students' learning outcomes and the efficiency of teachers and schools in producing them. This prevailing wisdom accepted that learning could be measured as an increase in the number of facts and procedures that a student has mastered.

Modern theories of learning, which emerged in the late 1950s, no longer reflect these simplistic models. Cognitive scientists describe learning as a process of learners dynamically making meaning out of new information in the context of their prior understanding. Facts and procedures, historical understanding, cultural references, and more are all important as building blocks for current and new understanding, but learning is more than simply building that knowledge base. The mind is constantly operating at the boundary between prior knowledge and new information, actively working to make meaning by applying, testing, and revising its rules and conceptual frameworks to account for the new information it's presented with. If this is how we conceive of learning, our models for teaching and assessment should surely shift toward a more student-centered model, whereby students actively construct and demonstrate their growing understanding.

I was lucky to have experienced this approach to learning as a student. I grew up in a small, conservative town in central New Jersey, where the schools were very traditional: desks in rows, a strong emphasis on phonics, and lots and lots of worksheets. Which is why I so vividly remember Mr. Fillmore, my seventh-grade science teacher. I was relieved to learn I had been assigned to Mr. Fillmore's class, because the other science teacher notoriously required students to memorize and recite the periodic table of elements. In contrast, Mr. Fillmore's approach to teaching science was rooted in discovery. When our class studied chemistry, Mr. Fillmore let us build a still, on our own, in the utility closet next to the classroom, where we produced white lightning for six weeks. (He never allowed us to taste it, claiming contact with the rubber stoppers rendered the spirit poisonous. Hmm.) Excited by the clandestine thrill, we applied ourselves to learning how yeast transformed grain into sugar and sugar into alcohol, and we learned to represent the process through chemical notations.

In another project, Mr. Fillmore directed my friend and me to develop a model of our city government. He set us up in the school office with a phone, a phonebook, and a pad of paper, and told us to collect data and come back with a plan for the town. Entirely on our own for a week, we called the city council, town administrators, the chamber of commerce, the police department, the fire department, and the city utilities. We asked them about their staffing and budgets. We looked at maps. We located parks, hospitals, and schools. We developed budgets and developed a plan for the town.

Looking back, what I remember most about Mr. Fillmore's class was the excitement of building new knowledge. We weren't just learning about something—we were creating something. And in the process, we were learning the scientific method, how to engineer an apparatus to effect a chemical process, math skills, financial literacy skills, organizational models, and how to talk effectively to adults. We worked in teams. We learned *with* one another.

Mr. Fillmore's class has shaped my own theories of learning and assessment. A well-constructed task *educes* (from the Latin *educere*, to lead or draw out) the learning by engaging the learner in discovery, analysis, consolidation of information, formation of a perspective, and argumentation to advance our shared understanding. All good curriculum, instruction, and assessment should engage students in this creative process of constructive, collective meaning-making. Assessments designed to support these more holistic learning models are typically more open-ended, requiring students to both formulate problems and demonstrate how to address them. Grading for extended classroom projects can also incorporate noncognitive dimensions of the task, including goal setting, self-management, and teamwork, all of which are highly correlated with broader measures of postsecondary success.

Many of these dimensions can be measured within the constraints of more standardized performance tasks, however. The International Baccalaureate Diploma Programme, for example, includes an extended essay—scored by external examiners—that requires students to formulate a research question, conduct research, analyze evidence, and support a position. New Meridian's assessments include scored performance tasks where students must analyze a simulated physical phenomenon in science, develop and defend a thesis based on synthesizing data from multiple sources, and rewrite a literary passage assuming the perspective of a secondary character. All of these more open-ended tasks require students to not simply provide an answer but to demonstrate the more complex thinking skills involved in developing an answer.

Recognize that Meaning-Making Is a Sociocultural Phenomenon

Meaning-making is also a socially and culturally embedded activity that reflects shared ways of thinking, knowing, and doing. We think collaboratively by building on one another's ideas. These ideas include our cultural assumptions. What are the implications for assessment if we believe reading and learning are socially and culturally mediated? Research in reading over the last forty years has established the importance of background knowledge as a significant contributor to reading ability.[5] We construct meaning from a text by first decoding individual words and then integrating the meaning of those words into our prior knowledge. If the background knowledge we bring to reading a text is socially and culturally specific, then our assessments will likely reflect those differences.[6] For instance, students from India or Pakistan might be better prepared to calculate the lengths of the sides of a triangle in the context of a cricket pitch than a baseball diamond. How should this inform our assessment design? Is the cultural context an advantage for students who have lived in cricket-playing countries? Or is it an appropriate way to make the test question more accessible to a specific student group?

These are vexing questions for test developers. Historically, the assessment field has prioritized the elimination of construct-irrelevant factors that might favor one student group over another, issuing long lists of topics and words that test writers should avoid. The performance of different student groups is rigorously analyzed for any systemic bias, carefully evaluating whether students of different genders, races or ethnicities, levels of English proficiency, and types of disabilities perform differently on each test question when controlling for overall performance on the test.

Statistically speaking, no modern standardized assessment should be biased toward any one student group over another.

Recognizing that meaning-making is socially and culturally mediated suggests that rather than trying to eliminate all possible sources of bias, it might be better to create tests that reflect and affirm the diversity of all our students. The hope is to offer a variety of culturally specific ways for students to demonstrate mastery by drawing on their diverse ways of thinking, knowing, and doing—without altering the underlying construct we're trying to measure. At New Meridian, we are currently experimenting with this by developing culturally relevant testlets that incorporate texts and traditions specific to Native American communities in Montana and Cajun communities in Louisiana. We are researching whether such assessments are more sensitive to measuring student reading comprehension skills when students report having greater familiarity with the cultural context.

Theoretically, such culturally differentiated assessments could hold promise for closing persistent test-score underperformance for historically underserved students. But significant challenges become immediately apparent: How do you define students' cultural identification to assign a culturally differentiated assessment? How finely do you differentiate culturally based test content? Do we develop culturally differentiated test forms for Southerners and Northerners? Catholics and Protestants? Republicans and Democrats? A special form just for California? Even when translating math assessments into Spanish, we struggle with differences in Spanish idioms and vocabulary among students from Mexico, Puerto Rico, and the Dominican Republic. If it's this challenging to translate a test based on different dialects of the same language, imagine how hard it will be to create different assessments for different communities.

Currently, standardized assessments don't support this kind of differentiation, so this is still an untested hypothesis. If we can develop more content-specific assessments aligned to the local curriculum, as well as the psychometric scoring methodologies required to equate culturally specific assessments into theta, we may be able to derive a reliable, comparable scale score from culturally differentiated assessments.

CONCLUSION

We have just lived through a historic moment in the US educational system. One might have expected this unprecedented crisis to have sparked unprecedented change. And yet the status quo in American schooling—which includes statewide accountability testing—has largely prevailed. Despite this inertia, change is happening. More than twenty states are currently piloting innovative assessment programs that seek to strike a better and more coherent balance between assessment of learning and assessment for learning. There is a new, shared conviction that tests must actually help students learn. I believe this is defining the future of assessment.

This will be no small feat. The technical differences between formative and summative assessments are very real. If, however, we can rethink these differences, we can free ourselves from faulty assumptions and binary approaches to what's required for classroom assessments versus statewide assessments. And in the process, we can build a system of assessments that reprioritizes learning; puts teachers, students, and families at the center of why we test; prepares students for the complexities of the twenty-first century; and maintains our moral obligation to ensure our schools are serving all students equitably.

This is a future worth striving for.

10

Confessions of an Education Publisher

Larry Berger and Alexandra Walsh

"Just tell us what it's like. People in DC don't know what education entrepreneurs do all day." It was 2006, and Rick Hess, an editor of this volume,
was convincing us to write an article about launching an education tech
startup. We weren't clear on why people would want to hear about our
daily slog, but getting paid a few dollars a page to vent was therapeutic and
good for the ramen supply.

So we described our wanderings through indifferent district offices,
forlorn education trade shows, and skeptical venture capital conference
rooms, as well as our toils to make formative assessment tools that ran on
a (cutting-edge at the time) Palm Pilot.

It turned out—as Rick had foreseen—that our tales of woe were illumi-
nating to those who were shaping policies to address educational innovation. The article he commissioned was cited as an input into the federal
Investing in Innovation and Race to the Top programs.

Four years later, our education startup was a few hundred people serving a few million students and their teachers. Some of that growth came
from getting better at what we were doing, but much of it was the state and
federal policies and philanthropic initiatives that were starting to stim-
ulate the market for education innovation. We used this momentum to

invest in more ambitious products and branched out from assessment to intervention, professional development, data systems, and more.

But there was one part of the market—core curriculum (what used to be called the textbook)—that we avoided. It worked by rules that were mysterious to us as entrepreneurs and to those in adjacent parts of education (policy, government, research) who were starting to rethink every other aspect of how schools work—but allowed the textbooks to continue gathering dust.

As a product category, the core curriculum has all the features that should attract entrepreneurs. It is the largest market in instructional materials, about $4 billion in the United States. It has the biggest mindshare among teachers, as it's a part of the daily routine in most classrooms. For this reason, it has the greatest opportunity, among instructional materials products, for educational impact. And it is ripe for innovation. Textbooks in the twenty-first century still look a lot like textbooks in the nineteenth.

Nevertheless, we all accepted that the Big Edu oligopoly—the giant companies that had been making textbooks for one hundred years or more—were protected by a moat of regulatory capture, compliance, and scale requirements that repelled new entrants.

So we focused on selling an innovative $9 product against other startups, while the Big Edu companies sold a $125 textbook program against each other. Occasionally, a publisher would buy a startup like ours and issue a press release about their deep commitment to innovation. But instead of helping the startup continue to build genuine demand for its product, the publisher would start giving it away "free with order," bundled with a textbook. This strategy helped Big Edu protect its textbook cash cow, but once the promising innovation had become a loss leader, it was no longer attractive for the publisher to keep investing in it. Eventually, the founders would quit, and the innovation would stall. Meanwhile, startups trying to establish a similar product were going out of business or pivoting because it is hard to compete on price when your competitors are giving out their product for free.

We believed that our products were becoming increasingly impactful and would become even more so if we could keep improving them. We didn't want them to end their days as free-with-order trinkets inside a textbook, so we went to extreme lengths to avoid getting acquired by Big Edu. In 2010, we found a global media company willing—based on their experience making big bets in Hollywood and cable TV—to make a big bet on our company, enabling us to make our run at a vision of core curriculum.

Now, in 2024, there is a lot of policy interest in high-quality instructional materials (HQIM), with core curriculum as the focus of that attention. But what are the barriers to new entrants and breakthroughs in quality and scale? And how might we dismantle or surmount those barriers?

Our progress as a core curriculum company in 2024 echoes our progress as an assessment company in 2007. We win often enough to know that we have a real shot at realizing our vision and bringing it to scale, but we lose to Big Edu enough that we are still the underdog. So, eighteen years after the original article, Rick Hess and colleagues invited us to write this companion piece about entering the territory of core curriculum.

Alexandra Walsh, who was in high school when that first article was published and is now Amplify's chief product officer, joins in describing our journey. Alexandra represents a new breed of education tech innovators, who grew up with digital technology in their own schooling and later made it intrinsic to their approach as teachers. She now runs a product research and development team of several hundred people working to build the future of instructional materials and to compete against Big Edu.

We will first describe the barriers to rethinking core curriculum, including obstacles that block new entrants and discourage existing players from innovating. Then, we will offer some reasons to hope that there could be a significant reinvention of core curriculum in the coming years.

WHAT IS A CORE CURRICULUM?

A core curriculum in a given subject has at least one lesson for every day of the school year. It covers 100 percent of the state standards in that subject and is often responsive to many other state and national compliance frameworks.

A full K–12 core curriculum in one subject can take the form of at least thirteen teacher editions (one for each grade), thirteen student editions, thirteen Spanish teacher and student editions, student workbooks in both languages, an assessment guide, and often a set of intervention resources for students who need additional support. For the early grades, there are kits of manipulatives, each the size of a breadbox. In English language arts (ELA), these are full of letter blocks, flashcards, and reading motivation posters; in science, colored pipe cleaners, solar panels, and rainforest soil for experiments; in math, number blocks, place value rods, and probability dice. In the paper versions of these programs, which are still necessary almost everywhere, the whole program runs to tens of thousands of pages. The shipment of boxes that arrives in a teacher's classroom is the size of a sofa. If you expect to win even 10 percent of the market, you need about a million square feet of warehouse space to store it all.

NINE BARRIERS TO TEXTBOOK INNOVATION

Below, we describe current barriers to market entry and success in core curriculum as we have experienced them.

Money

Making a core curriculum requires a bit of masochism, a willingness to be responsible for cutting down millions of trees, and—one hopes—a reverence for the power of a good curriculum to support and perhaps inspire excellent teaching and learning. It also requires a huge pile of cash. A rule of thumb is that the mainstream players who get substantial market share will spend at least $150 million creating a new K–12 program in one subject. Some niche players and nonprofits spend less, but that number is still in the tens of millions. We are currently watching nonprofit players who raised less than this amount circling back to major funders for a third or fourth round of investment, hoping to make themselves sustainable.

If you want to be an enduring player in the core curriculum market, and not just a one-hit wonder who ends up needing to distribute your product through an incumbent, then it will likely cost at least $400 million to get started. To explain why, it helps to meet Louise, a former star salesperson at one of the Big Edu companies, who explained the price tag to us.

We knew about Louise because people had warned us that it might not be worth trying to sell our first core product, an ELA program, in

Louise's territory. Nobody could beat her. And indeed, it took her only a few rhetorical questions to sway her loyal customers away from Amplify. She would stand before a curriculum selection committee and say, "Have you seen Amplify's ELA program? It's so impressive. Such cool software. It's like it is from the future." It almost seemed she was pitching us. But then she started thinking out loud: "I wonder what happens when your Wi-Fi network goes down? Has the network ever gone down in your classroom? Who wants to share a time when their network went down?" That was game over for Amplify. We learned the hard way that to win in most districts, we needed to ship both a print program and a digital program. It was too late for the first edition of our ELA program, but we were already stockpiling glossy paper and colored ink for our science program.

Since we couldn't beat Louise, we decided we might try to recruit her in time for the science adoptions. She sighed and shifted into her remedial teacher voice to explain why that wouldn't work: "It looks like your science program might be good enough to beat me (though don't count on it). But I haven't heard anything about Amplify launching a math program. The place I'm working has two science programs and five math programs. And then there's the social studies adoption. If I join you just for science, it will be five years after that until the next ELA adoption. In my current job, I've got a big-ticket item to sell every two years."

We were able to recruit Louise by revealing that we did have stealth plans to build a math program. Had Amplify lacked the capital or team to do so, we would have lost her. Years later, Louise's winning streak continues—only now, she racks up these wins at our company.

Our experience with Louise demonstrates that to have a healthy sales channel, a core curriculum player needs to play in at least three subjects. This means an up-front investment of at least $400 million. And Louise and her colleagues don't come cheap—a small national sales force and a credible marketing team costs another $30 million or more per year. Double that because they expect to be on the ground "setting the agenda" two or three years before the sale happens.

Several hundred million is a lot to invest in a high-risk venture. Ordinary venture capital and private equity companies have avoided doing so. Pharmaceutical companies make bets of that scale, but only when it looks like a drug has a good shot at winning a multibillion-dollar global market. In core curriculum, there is no international market, and you have no way of knowing if you are likely to win before you've made the investment.

Which brings us to the next barrier . . .

Time and Timing

If you want to make a room of humorless venture capitalists laugh, try this elevator pitch:

"Good morning. We want to launch a core curriculum company."
"Isn't that expensive?"
"Let's get to cost later."
"Okay, then tell us about the early traction you are seeing."
"We don't have any traction yet."
"When will you know if you have traction?"
"In eight years."

Cue laughter from the venture capitalists. And keep in mind that you haven't even told them how much it will cost.

Most venture investors think in terms of five- to seven-year windows for the investment to be sold or go public, which means that even if the financing were available, a core curriculum company doesn't have time to show its worth before venture capitalists seek greener pastures.

Core curriculum is expensive and slow. It takes four or five years to author, design, and produce the tens of thousands of pages and corresponding software required to build it. If you are a new entrant with unproven products published under an unfamiliar brand, it will take three to four years for most customers to be willing to take a risk with you, and it will take you *at least* that long to refine your product-market fit. So that is eight years for a single product, which means getting established in three subjects will generally take ten or more. The big publishers have been at this for a hundred years, which gives them a head start of back-catalog materials that can be recycled into new programs. And, because they lack stiff competition, they have accumulated vast reserves of cash and confidence with which to make these investments.

The only reason we were able to enter this market is that a media company, which was larger than the big publishers, backed us for four years. By then, we had found a remarkable group of long-term, impact-oriented investors who were willing to back us for another six years until the business started to break even on an annual basis. Our case is lucky and rare.

The timeframes described above assume that the states and districts buy the product on the schedule they announce years in advance. But states often decide to delay adoption or change the requirements for doing so. Or cancel it outright. Or move it up a year. The cost of each of these moves is astronomical for the bidders in these adoptions, especially if the publisher has already printed the materials with the copyright year or with the standards that have now changed. It is an equally big disaster when a state calls the adoption early, because this often means that the publisher has not finished building a program and therefore doesn't have time to submit it.

The impact of these schedule changes on the companies in the market does not seem to be on the radar of policymakers. Established publishers have the cash to weather these shifts and decades of experience in contingency planning. But large swings in timing can cause smaller competitors to publish and then perish without ever getting a chance to compete.

Committees

There is a confession attributed to a big textbook publisher:

> I don't write textbooks for students because students don't buy textbooks. I also don't write textbooks for teachers because teachers don't buy textbooks. I write textbooks for committees because committees buy textbooks.

Unlike any other procurement process in education, core curriculum decisions are made by committees made up primarily of teachers. Sometimes, as in Waukegan, Illinois, the whole town gets to vote, not just the educators. Occasionally, there is a student, an academic expert, or a parent on the committee. Sometimes, it consists of all the teachers in a district. But most of the time, it is a group of between eight and eighty teachers who have volunteered for or been appointed to the committee.

We were well into building curriculum before people started to explain the phenomenon of these committees. And we were selling for at least a year before we fully grasped the power and peculiarity of having these committees as our customers. All of the previous products we sold were primarily bought by a decision-maker in the central office. If you had a good meeting with the right person, often the superintendent or the chief academic officer (CAO), you might be on track for a sale. So we kept doing this vestigial activity—visiting central offices, meeting with leaders, and demonstrating our curriculum to them. But even when we had a great meeting, nothing would happen as a result. The superintendent or the CAO wouldn't presume to assert an opinion about core curriculum or put pressure on the teacher committee.

We have come to like the democracy and practicality of the committee process in which each member gets a vote. Most participants on most committees show remarkable dedication to reading hundreds of pages of each program, exploring the software, and trying it in class with their students. And they generally aren't paid any extra by their district to do all of this. One or two may be there to voice a political or religious position more than a pedagogical one. Still, all take seriously the responsibility of choosing the curriculum they and their peers will use for the next several years. They are not susceptible to guru authors, grandiose claims, or fancy features that attempt to conceal weak lessons. Ultimately, teacher-led decisions about core curriculum can get widespread buy-in from the rest of the teachers in a district in ways that top-down central office decisions rarely do.

While we have learned to stop worrying and love the teacher committees, we do keep an eye on the way that they exert pressures that can push one's products toward compromise and mediocrity. If half the room intensely loves your core curriculum program and half the room intensely hates it, committee dynamics will likely cause you to lose to the program that everyone tepidly tolerates. As soon as you think of your audience as a committee, there is pressure to write more defensively—with an eye toward the impossible goal of pleasing everyone.

The only antidote to this is having a sales and support team that is on the ground in the district, responding to each teacher's concerns, answering every question, and committing to a lot of hand-holding, customization, and change management during implementation so that the committee feels empowered to make an ambitious choice. Of course, having a team that can do this kind of custom work at scale is yet another barrier to a new entrant.

Flip Tests and Caravans

Some committees spend months poring over the proposed instructional materials. Many districts even do full-year pilots of the top two or three choices. A few committees look at not only which program teachers like but also relevant academic research and analyses.

But a great many others make their decision based on a five-minute ritual called *the flip test*—picking up the book, flipping through the pages, and never looking at the digital experience for teachers and students.

Then there are the *caravans*, in which districts give each competing publisher equal time in a rapid sequence. These show-and-tells are usually preposterously short: our salespeople tell stories of having to present an entire K–8 curriculum in fifteen minutes. While caravans have become less common, around 20 percent of states still do them. Some still have caravans where there is no formal presentation—publishers just set up booths and teachers decide whom to invite to their district based on a flip test and a brief conversation with a sales rep.

Flip tests and caravans favor print over digital. It takes time to explore what makes a digital program work. You need to use it with students to see the power of classroom orchestration, dynamic grouping and differentiation, and tools that save time on feedback and grading.

Cursory reviews also mean that instructionally rich programs with comprehensive materials for teacher support often lose to the cutest illustrations and the glossiest covers. The British educator Hugh Burkhardt once asked us, "Why are American textbooks designed to look like a clown exploded on every page?" The answer has much to do with trying to capture attention during the flip test. Teachers used to frown as they flipped through our black-and-white samples and compared them to the familiar and colorful basal readers from the big publishers. It took years of losing with our relatively complicated Core Knowledge Language Arts curriculum before we finally broke into the market with a boost from the science of reading movement, a lot more color, and the introduction of an adorable talking grasshopper.

If one curriculum's lessons have moments of subtlety or surprise, the flip test and the caravan will pass them over.

Standards and the Politics of Standards

It would be impractical and expensive to run a national railroad if the track gauge differed in every state. Imagine Indiana claiming its railroad tracks are a groundbreaking fifty-three inches apart, whereas Illinois is a pathetic fifty-six inches. There would be no material improvement in how a train would run. On the contrary, there would be train wrecks and wasteful stops at the border to adjust the wheels in every state. Citizens across the country would object or stop taking trains.

Over the last decade, it has become politically fashionable for states to abandon common standards in ELA and math. States are proud of their idiosyncratic standards even when they do not really differ in meaningful ways from those of other states. If one state teaches magnetism in fifth grade and another teaches it in third grade, then curriculum materials designed for one are written at the wrong reading level for the other. But there is usually no substantial pedagogical argument for choosing one over the other. Divergence of standards requires core publishers to create multiple versions of their programs with only slight differences. Economies of scale collapse, and vendors inevitably pass along the increased costs to the schools. The waste adds up to hundreds of millions of dollars in effort and diverts spending from more valuable activities, like research and development and teacher support.

This also means that some publishers decide not to compete in small states with unique standards. These states miss out on state-of-the-art products and get nothing in return.

Our point is not to make the case for any particular common standards effort, just that there should be one, or at most a few groups of states with overlapping standards. This would enable a new entrant to build one program that addresses a broad market rather than favoring incumbents that already have a catalog of different programs. The incumbents also have a big enough sales force in each state to make it worthwhile to do all the customization.

Forbidden Improvement

Before a district decides to adopt new materials, train their teachers, and build up infrastructure around a curriculum, they typically want assurances that major chunks of content won't go away or change dramatically overnight. For example, if you purchase a curriculum with a unit on *Charlotte's Web*, it would be challenging if Charlotte and Wilbur disappeared in year three of your adoption. Teachers would need to be retrained, local assessments might need to be revised, and lesson modifications that teachers had designed might become obsolete.

To avoid these problems, some states and school systems instituted ironclad contracts and regulatory systems. Though the intentions were good, in practice these contractual requirements block improvement. If we get consistent feedback that some parts of an instructional sequence—the writing assignments in the unit on *Charlotte's Web*, for example—are confusing or not challenging enough, we are prohibited from changing them for the entire duration of the adoption. If a group of teachers figures out how to improve one of our lessons, we can't update it so all teachers can benefit. In some states, we can't even introduce an optional set of writing prompts in response to user feedback and student performance data.

Some districts adopt for eight to ten years. There are few other product categories in which the customer desires, and even mandates, no improvements for an entire decade. It is therefore unsurprising that teachers often want to switch providers the next time they adopt materials. In many cases, their provider's curriculum was not as good as it could have been because the provider did not have the opportunity to make the product better.

Requirements for a static curriculum made more sense in the world of print textbooks. However, in the world of a digital or blended curriculum, the constraint can become absurd. Instead of having one best version of the content and the software, bolstered by regular updates, these policies prevent teachers and students from accessing the latest and greatest version of the product and create a lot of additional expense as each vendor maintains old versions of their product.

Fragmented Implementation

In the print textbook world, there was not much to learn about how to use the curriculum you had just purchased. It was a book, and you already know how to use a book. Maybe you needed a quick summary of what was different about the pedagogical routines in this book, and you may have cared what else was "free with order" in the box, but it did not take hours of training to become a user. In the world of HQIM and digital or blended curricula, the learning curve is steeper, and the rewards of becoming a power user are greater. District policies have not changed to meet the evolving challenges of implementation.

There is an outdated expectation that publishers should include one free day of "unboxing" professional development up front and then walk away from the implementation. Districts prefer to source additional training, coaching, and change management, if any, from dedicated professional learning providers or local retired educators. However, those providers often do not understand the nuances of particular curricula and may be unable to answer any questions about the tech platform that powers the newer programs.

It is especially problematic that publisher professional services are perceived as lower quality. While that might have been true historically, and may still be an issue in some cases, companies that have dedicated the time to building strong curriculum materials have also focused intensely on what is needed for implementation success.

Not only can many of the HQIM providers deliver strong training, they can also provide customers access to the team that authored the curriculum and designed the software. We have established dedicated channels on our company Slack channel for questions from our professional services team. Program authors and content team members are on standby to answer big and small questions. This kind of access is not possible if a district uses an outside professional development partner during implementation. And providing ongoing professional learning support is a key input to improving the product over time by addressing the places where teachers are experiencing confusion.

Instructional Incoherence

Core curriculum is central to classroom instruction, but it is just one small part of the constellation of instructional materials, tools, and systems that districts must purchase. As teacher committees are picking core programs, district chief technology officers are choosing learning management systems, special education coordinators are picking intervention programs, and states are mandating assessments. Then there are hundreds of supplemental resources from websites like Pinterest, Teachers Pay Teachers, and Khan Academy that individual teachers cobble together to boost student engagement and fill real or perceived gaps in core instruction. Often, the assessments match with none of the above.

Educators should be free to make heterogeneous choices about what works for their kids, but they often expect that these divergent resources will work with one another. We have ambitious roadmaps for all that we would like to do to improve our products, but we end up spending a disproportionate amount of our development capacity on third-party integrations and retrofitting our programs to work with the collection of outside tools and products the district has purchased.

Current learning management systems (LMS) are designed to support all content areas and be content-agnostic. We understand the appeal of a single platform across the district, but the uniformity means that they are not attuned to the content of any particular program. As a result, the interface we've designed to make students feel like they are ice scientists solving a complex engineering problem or detectives deciphering an Edgar Allan Poe mystery is homogenized into the same LMS interface used for every other subject in K–12 and often higher education. And the LMSs entirely collapse when it comes to integrating bespoke pedagogical software that is responsive in the moment to what is happening in the classroom.

HOPE FOR THE FUTURE

The long list of barriers we have just described may seem forbidding. Decades of unsuccessful challenges to established publishers confirm that they are real and formidable.

However, incremental changes are afoot, and there is growing energy and hope in the sector. It is in the nature of entrepreneurship to see openings where others see obstacles and to probe the vulnerabilities in barriers that make them surmountable. We see shifts in policy and demand that could favor innovation over the status quo. Some startups and upstarts are getting early traction. And core curriculum remains the place to play if you want to have a significant impact on student outcomes, so the worlds of policy and practice are increasingly focused on it.

Here are four reasons we are hopeful.

The HQIM Movement

Concern about the outdated, nonrigorous, misaligned core curriculum products used in the early 2000s led to the HQIM movement, which has growing traction in almost every state. It has created quality ratings and guidance—from places such as EdReports, Student Achievement Partners, KnowledgeWorks, and others—in a market that was previously driven by familiar brands, marketing claims, and compliance. Probably the biggest reason Amplify Science was able to get noticed as an upstart program was that it was rated "meets expectations" on EdReports before any other program.

The HQIM movement is about more than rating programs. It is also about organizing instruction around the core curriculum so that learning can progress coherently. It also puts more focus on students doing grade-level work rather than getting trapped in a cycle of remediation. Too many schools were drifting into a reductive system that focused on remediating assessment results rather than providing students with the curricular supports that might help them access grade-level work and a deeper sense of the disciplines they are studying. The more schools organize around the core curriculum, the more developers can focus on the excellence of their products rather than on integrating with all the other parts of the system.

Visionary States

Often, education policy at the state level drives HQIM practices at the district level. A growing number of states have begun to redesign their core curriculum procurement and support systems to focus on product quality and rigorous implementation.

Louisiana, for example, doesn't just list compliant programs. It ranks them as tier one, tier two, and tier three, so that districts are aware of which programs are more research-based and aligned to standards than others. The state also commits substantial resources to building capacity in districts that choose a tier one program. If they choose tier one, they join a community of other districts implementing the same program and receive intensive training and support that is provided or subsidized by the state.

Louisiana also provides grant dollars for high-quality materials *and* requires that districts include robust professional learning plans in those grants. Professional development has to stretch beyond the traditional unboxing training and into deep engagements with the product to improve implementation and teacher practice. Louisiana is even experimenting with redesigning their high-stakes assessments to better align with the content of the state's preferred curriculum choices.

There are other states taking bold action on curriculum, including Texas, which is ensuring that districts have funding to purchase high-quality materials annually instead of having to wait every eight years, as they have historically. In addition, the Council of Chief State School Officers' High-Quality Instructional Materials and Professional Development Network started with eight states and now includes thirteen. In other words, this movement is growing, and we believe the innovation in those states may allow publishers to develop deep partnerships over long periods of time, which will help them push for real impact.

Open Educational Resources and Free Curriculum Materials

Over the past decade, various efforts, usually funded by a combination of philanthropy and state government, have enabled the creation of core curriculum materials shared under Open Educational Resources (OER) licenses. This approach can reduce barriers to entry for new entrants in the market and for schools to gain access.

It may seem counterintuitive that freely available resources are becoming drivers of business growth, but decades ago, Stuart Brand described the current predicament well when he said, "Information wants to be free. Information also wants to be expensive."[1] OER programs are making it easy to freely access a high-quality curriculum, which provides an opportunity for vendors like Amplify to add proprietary value by rendering it in both print and digital, adding tools, providing customer support, and improving the product over time. In most cases, the commercial versions of these programs are as expensive as the competition—often because the OER programs are more comprehensive, and the value-added tools have to be especially good to get districts to buy rather than just use the free version.

Two of Amplify's core curriculum products are OER-based: Amplify Core Knowledge Language Arts and Amplify Desmos Math. It was initially challenging to convince our sales teams they would still have something to sell if we or our partners posted a full program for free online. However, our reps bought in after seeing the way it changed the dynamics of the teacher committees. Instead of entering a teacher committee with an unknown product, our reps are entering a roomful of fans who have already tried the free versions with their students.

Before a district is ready to buy a core program, teachers might be ready to try something new *and* free. OER content enables teachers to try something new without the bureaucracy associated with full-district procurement and implementation. And OER products are often supported by an infrastructure of strong professional development providers and philanthropists.

Not only is our math product based on an admired OER Math offering, large chunks of it are available to try for free via our software platform, Desmos Classroom. We work hard to build communities around our free products. We use social media, webinars, and other tools to support communities of teachers who make these products part of their collective identities. Teachers become power users of the Desmos tools and the Amplify-Desmos math content years before an opportunity for formal adoption appears. We have enthusiastic educators begging their districts to run an adoption process. (This is unprecedented.)

So, instead of "I write textbooks for committees because committees buy textbooks," we now focus on getting teachers on board steadily over time, often by showing them software, tools, and more beautiful print versions of the product they already like in its downloadable form. It is a much longer investment, but it builds a deeper relationship and fosters a dynamic where the best product for teachers and students—not the product most friendly to committee consensus—has a chance to win.

Emerging Demand for Coherence

The typical teacher supply closet is heterogeneous—shelves of books from a wide assortment of publishers, plus puzzles, activities, experiments, workbooks, modules, games, and posters sourced from wherever they can be found. Two separately authored Houghton Mifflin Harcourt storybooks don't have any compatibility advantage over one Houghton Mifflin Harcourt and one Random House storybook.

Software is different. Two pieces of software can become more valuable by talking to each other, especially if one was designed with the other in mind. They can have a common login and user interface as well as a shared place where files and data are stored. This saves time and hassle for teachers and provides them with tools to better understand what and how their students are learning.

The pandemic dramatically expanded the use of software for curriculum. All but the most skeptical teachers found software that is now essential to their work. But teachers want the different pieces of software to talk to one another and to be more responsive to *what* they are teaching. Teachers are exasperated by having multiple passwords, various places where student work is filed, different user interfaces, and misaligned pedagogies and instructional sequences.

We hear teachers asking for four kinds of coherence that are elusive in the current education market:

- *Pedagogical coherence.* The way students are taught in different instructional materials should be aligned and grounded in the best research about teaching and learning.

- *Content coherence.* The curriculum, assessments, and intervention materials should be integrated. Assessments should measure what is being taught. The system should be making remediation recommendations and offering support that is aligned with what students are doing right now in the curriculum. The intervention resources should be preparing students for tomorrow's lesson.
- *Data coherence.* The data from assessments, personalized learning software, classwork, homework, essays, and projects should feed one common data store with robust tools for analysis at the student, class, and system levels. This will increasingly mean that the data embedded in learning experiences can do some of the work that discreet assessments do today and reduce the need for testing.
- *Experiential coherence.* Teachers want one login; a common interface from product to product; student work, teacher notes, and resources stored in consistent places; and print and digital versions fully aligned. Ideally, it would all be organized around supporting teachers as they navigate the different parts of their day, from prepping for class, to leading discussion, to grading, to communicating with parents, to interacting with other educators.

Teacher committees that purchase core curricula are beginning to look for this kind of coherence. Eventually, state and district policy will follow the teachers' leads such that evaluation of these characteristics will replace the dreary compliance that defines most core curriculum procurements today.

In the rare moments in education when the demand side changes dramatically, old barriers to entry often shift or topple. To address the demand for coherence, many of the players in education, old and new, are attempting to assemble or collaborate on integrated systems of core curriculum, supplemental materials, assessment, professional learning, and data analysis. No one has a fully realized version of this yet, but the race is on, and new players may have fewer internal barriers to achieving this vision than incumbents.

This demand for coherence goes beyond software integration. Most educators believe that classroom life—teachers interacting with students,

students interacting with one another, students interacting with learning experiences, and so forth—should be more seamless. To help create more relationship-focused classrooms, some of the most promising products responding to the demands for coherence don't require putting a screen in front of children. The more coherent the experience, the more the software can be in the background, which helps teachers and students make the most of human connection.

CONCLUSION

In most places, little has changed in the policies and procurement processes that have bought textbooks for decades. But change is steadily coming. Some states are becoming more focused on quality. New communities of users and innovators are springing up around open educational resources. New kinds of programs are starting to win the old procurements by responding to teacher demand for greater coherence.

These changes seem significant enough that they may, in turn, start to change what future procurements request. There is reason to hope that we will soon see:

- a more diverse supply of new core curriculum products competing on quality and innovation;
- a renaissance of teacher enthusiasm and inventiveness that enables teachers to tune instruction to their students and to rethink teaching and learning;
- revised procurement policies that make it easier for schools to invest in these products and the services that help teachers use them well;
- a breakthrough in student achievement, growth, and motivation.

For those searching for a place in education that is ripe for rethinking, where longstanding barriers to innovation are more vulnerable than they have been in decades, core curriculum may be the textbook case.

Conclusion

REINVENTION IN PRACTICE

Frederick M. Hess, Michael B. Horn,
and Juliet Squire

This book is rooted in our conviction that the work of reinventing American education starts with rethinking what's possible but is ultimately a matter of what happens on the ground. The sector is rife with visions for the future of teaching and learning. Some reinvigorate old methods of instruction, such as inquiry-based learning; others seek to unlock new technologies to build futuristic experiences. The three of us have each written about what ambitious reinventions could look like. But this abundance of vision can go nowhere without a commensurate focus on what it takes to translate these ideas into practice.

What does it take to use time, talent, and technology in more powerful ways? How do we make the student experience more personal, rigorous, and engaging? What does it look like to ensure that assessment is about measuring competencies rather than batch-processing students and that curricula are designed to build mastery rather than fill a designated number of instructional days?

The answers to such questions are not uniform. And an unfortunate, if understandable, reality is that those who have the most insight into these puzzles tend to be far removed from analysis and policymaking. Why? It's because they're busy doing this work.

Analysts, academics, and advocates tend to focus on the conceptual rather than the concrete. We often talk and write in terms of analogies and intriguing examples rather than the day-to-day hassles of, say, negotiating with teacher unions or pitching products to curriculum committees. This has predictable consequences. It means there's often a lot more attention paid to policy (something that we scribblers can claim to influence) than to the messy realities of practice.

This book is one attempt to help address that imbalance. Our aim is to put the spotlight on those who've been busy doing this work and give them an opportunity to share practical takeaways, challenges, opportunities, and lessons they've learned. The result speaks for itself: a series of essays that gives an in-the-trenches view of what reinvention really looks like. This final chapter distills five of the insights that jumped out to us from across the contributions: get clear on what's changing and why, remember that successes often start small and change as they scale, take things as they come, focus on the human aspects of the system, and turn to policy when there's no other way forward.

BROAD TAKEAWAYS

Get Clear on What's Changing and Why

Several authors noted that, all too often in schools, we don't spend enough time clarifying the problem being solved or what precisely will change—and why. This lack of common understanding can easily stymie improvement efforts. The importance of gaining clarity on what's changing and why comes across in several ways.

To precisely identify problems and potential solutions, it helps to have a shared vocabulary. Beth Rabbitt, for example, makes a point about the role of language that's important, if easy to overlook. The words we use shape the way we think. Readers are probably used to this point being made in a more ideological context by advocates with agendas. But Beth's point is simpler and more compelling. She notes that in partnering with one California school district that sought to combat abysmal academic achievement by embracing performance-based learning, it was crucial to shift away from the terms *student* and *teacher* and toward *learner* and *fa-*

cilitator. Why? Because words like *student* and *teacher* embody a bunch of learned behaviors, assumptions, routines, and expectations. Trying to change all that without being more precise with language was a recipe for confusion and frustration.

Now, it's easy to overestimate the importance of vocabulary. Education's long history of faddism has shown that it's easy to get caught up in verbiage and lose sight of substance. But it's tough to rethink productively if we're not clear about what we're trying to change, and that requires clear and precise language. Beth makes a related point when it comes to the change process. She quotes former Distinctive Schools CEO Scott Frauenheim observing, "Given how much success we'd had, and how much enthusiasm there was in other grades, I thought taking the tools the pilot team had developed to additional teams would be easy. . . . But it wasn't the tools the new teams needed: it was a version of the design process itself. We realized they needed to go through their own learning, aligned to a 'why,' to be able to use the tools now available in our system." Again, it's easy to get caught up in terminology or tools, but a persistent theme we encounter in these pages is the importance of getting clear on what's changing—and what it'll take to make that change successful.

Scott Ellis makes a similar point in his mastery learning chapter, where he argues that it's critical to have a shared understanding of what is being implemented and what the goal is. This means, he argues, that it's not enough to just say the words "mastery learning." Teachers need to understand what mastery is for each objective and that students are either "ready to move on to a new learning objective or they need to keep working on the current one." Arthur VanderVeen's chapter offers a case study on the importance of clarifying what we're asking assessment to do and represent.

Adam Peshek contends that although compromise can be critical to moving policies forward, it's important to be clear about what the end goal is. He notes that the desired result is not a specific policy but what the policy enables. All too often, we've noticed that advocates for rethinking education get stuck thinking it's their way or the highway, and they forget that there are a variety of ways to accomplish goals for students.

Take Things as They Come

Adam's reminder that compromise can be an important tool for progress raises another point that comes across in several chapters. Actually reinventing education is hard, and it's folly to try to do everything all at once. Staging change—no matter how you tackle it—is important.

Larry Berger and Alexandra Walsh's chapter puts a fine point on just how hard it is to reinvent schooling. One of the underappreciated challenges of education reform, as we've noted, is that dreaming up the perfect curriculum or new ways to do schooling is fun and relatively easy, whereas actually implementing such visions is another story. The dreamers tend to ignore just how high the barriers to entry and real change are. Larry and Alexandra point out that education has many stakeholders and that decisions are often made by committee. All of these stakeholders have a say, which raises the cost of change.

As Larry and Alexandra tell the tale of what it takes to sell to committees, they vividly illustrate the difference between dreaming up promising ideas and actually delivering on them. As they write, "If half the room intensely loves your core curriculum program and half the room intensely hates it, committee dynamics will likely cause you to lose to the program that everyone tepidly tolerates. As soon as you think of your audience as a committee, there is pressure to write more defensively—with an eye toward the impossible goal of pleasing everyone." The work of change is hard, expensive, and exhausting.

As a result, it's important to focus on what you can control. One of the things this volume makes clear is how much improvement is possible under today's conditions. Rick has written about this at length in his *Cage-Busting Teacher* and *Cage-Busting Leadership* books. And while this shouldn't serve as an excuse to ignore problematic laws or policies, it does suggest that much more energy should be devoted to tackling challenges that can already be addressed within existing structures. Amid all the hand-wringing about staffing shortages and teacher pay, for example, Brent Maddin makes clear that there are ways to do better even without new statutes or funding streams. Joel Rose advocates strongly for new assessment policies, but his success also illustrates that it's possible to redesign and accelerate math learning without waiting on ambitious new policy agendas.

This type of rethinking requires a commitment to taking advantage of existing levers rather than imagining how much better things could be in a perfect world. Waiting for things outside of your control to change is ultimately an exercise in procrastination, not reinvention. And, as the contributors make clear time and again, once you start looking at the things we can control, there are many more opportunities for improvement than might at first be apparent. This brings to mind the eighty-plus-year-old Serenity Prayer: "God grant me the serenity to accept the things I cannot change; courage to change the things I can; and wisdom to know the difference." Although rethinkers don't have to passively accept the status quo, it certainly helps to know the levers already at your disposal and start your work there.

Remember That Successes Often Start Small and Change as They Scale

An outgrowth of the wisdom of not doing everything all at once is Michael McShane's advice for small schools: doing one small thing well is critical before you can think about scale. As Michael observes, "Paradoxically, the path to scale might not be aiming for it immediately, but rather nurturing numerous smaller attempts to create great learning environments, some of which might scale and some of which might not."

Indeed, in perusing the assembled chapters, we were reminded that when people hear the stories of "disruptive innovations" or other massive transformations, there's a tendency to focus on the ending: a now-mature upstart innovation upends the forces of the status quo. But what they miss is that these transformations take a long time and rarely, if ever, see their initial successful design remain the same as it scales. It's only through steady improvement and lots of hard work to solve different types of problems in different contexts that disruptive innovations succeed in other areas and grow to replace the old ways of doing things. And that road of improvement is rarely a straight line forward.

This knowledge offers some useful lessons for education. As our authors make clear, many of the innovations we read about in these chapters—

mastery learning, personalization, AI, and more—have solved problems in specific circumstances. Their implementations were rarely straightforward as they were adapted to different contexts, problems, and priorities. The lesson shouldn't be, "Let's just do exactly what they did and apply it everywhere." That's too simplistic. Merely copying something step by step in one circumstance is unlikely to work elsewhere. What's more, oftentimes new practices work initially because of the Hawthorne effect—the tendency of folks to perform better or change behavior when they know they are under the microscope. But then those results fade over time. Instead of trying to scale the *what*, we need to look at the underlying principles of *why* successful rethinking has stood the test of time—and then accordingly adapt and improve the *what* to solve problems in different circumstances.

More generally, the concept of scale in education—a notion that often takes its cues from the world of software engineering, where we essentially copy and paste millions of lines of code to scale up applications—strikes us as problematic or remarkably incomplete. When it comes to education, the challenge of scale is much more like that in civil engineering than in software or manufacturing. The principles of physics remain the same from location to location, but how you apply those principles and build a bridge in earthquake-prone San Francisco is very different from how you would do it in snowy Buffalo. In other words, the specifics matter. Blindly copying practices without modifying them as you scale and things change isn't a recipe for success.

Focus on the Human Aspects of the System

That insight brings us to a fourth lesson that emerges from the chapters: human beings matter. It's impossible to get education right without them.

It's easy to get caught in conceptual shifts and aspirations without thinking of the people affected. However, the contributors remind us time and again how much depends on what these changes mean for students, parents, and educators. When it comes to mastery learning, for instance, Scott Ellis notes how often success depends on "unexpected but necessary changes in the basic steps of teaching and learning, like the importance of teachers taking time before starting new content to be sure students understand what they are learning and why it matters." He tells of a middle school math teacher who found that some of his "best students" struggled after the shift to mastery learning. The teacher observed that "these students were 'good at school' because they responded well to direction and did what they were told," but they floundered absent that guidance.

Scott recalls the math teacher relating that one of those students flatly told him, "I would appreciate it if you would just tell me what to do." High-level rethinkers don't usually expect such reactions from students. But on-the-ground reinventors recognize and adapt to the practical implications for individuals. Scott observes that similar challenges can arise with parents, "especially since so many aspects of the new approach differ from how parents learned themselves." That requires conscious attention to how this will play out for learners, educators, and parents alike. For instance, he writes:

> One of my clients at a large international elementary school in Singapore told me how much mastery learning changed the parent-teacher conference experience. . . . When the teacher described the student's performance at the parent-teacher conference, the parent bluntly said to the teacher, "Well, that must be because you are doing something wrong." The next year in their parent-teacher conference, the same teacher shared a mastery dashboard with the same parent and showed the specific learning objectives their child had not yet mastered. The parent reviewed the data, paused, turned to the student, and said, "Well, I guess now we know what to work on at home tonight."

The upshot is that these shifts are rarely just about changing pedagogy, assessment, or what have you. They also require paying deliberate attention to the expectations and routines of learners, educators, and parents.

Like it or not, that's a big part of what our contributors do every day. This is especially true with AI, which requires ensuring that the human dimension of this work is always front and center. Sal Khan, Kristen DiCerbo, and Rachel Boroditsky offer a terrific illustration of what this looks like when they discuss what it takes for AI tutoring to deliver on this promise. They observe that, "To really act like a human tutor, interactions with a generative AI should create a sense of familiarity, as if the tutor understands the student." For a student who is learning about probabilities and is passionate about soccer, an AI tutor "provides extra support for solving the problem" and "seamlessly tailors the problem to revolve around the likelihood of your favorite team winning the World Cup."

That same logic can be extended in all kinds of ways. For an aspiring veterinarian, "The next time you are faced with a fractions problem and question its practicality, your [AI] tutor might illustrate how understanding fractions relates to adjusting medical dosages to treat dogs of different sizes and give you a challenging problem in that context." Evident here is a disciplined commitment to thinking about students as people rather than as digital consumers. That mindset extends to the AI tutor, which was engineered as "an extremely qualified, kind, experienced, encouraging, patient, empathetic, and flexible tutor." The tutor says "I don't know" if unsure how to respond and relies on a Socratic approach to prompt reflection. Sure, this is all "innovative" in the sense that it's new and noteworthy, but it's defined by a focus on teaching and learning—not the underlying technology. In other words, AI is getting us back to basics.

Along those lines, it's clear that the teaching job itself is ripe for rethinking—which requires a focus on the human beings at the center of teaching and learning. Over the past half century, most efforts to improve teaching have taken the teacher's role as a given and then adopted a "more, better" response—seeking to give teachers more training, pay them more, or hire more teachers. Notable in the preceding chapters is the degree to which the contributors imply the need for a more fundamental rethinking of what teachers do and how they do it. Nowhere is this clearer than in Brent Maddin's chapter, where he explores the Next Education Workforce model. In making the case for this kind of redesign, Brent focuses on much more than achievement scores. He notes that teachers in team-based staffing models report "significant[ly] higher levels of self-efficacy and better relationships with students." His chapter also reveals that the team-based model makes teachers "more likely to recommend teaching to a friend or family member" and "more likely to be retained as teachers in the district in the following year." Brent also notes that educators in these programs take off fewer days and have higher evaluation scores than their one teacher, one classroom counterparts.

This all makes a fair bit of intuitive sense, as the limitations of the traditional model are all too familiar. And Brent's description of how teachers can operate under team-based approaches can seem frighteningly commonsensical:

> Ms. Adams is a third-grade teacher with fifteen years of experience. She is a great reading teacher but has admitted on occasion that she "isn't really a math person." She is a collaborator and a natural leader who is looking to earn a bit more money and have a greater impact, but she doesn't really want to be an administrator. . . . Mr. Harris *is* a math person. In fact, for the last ten years he worked as an electrical engineer, but he recently moved to a new community and struggled to find work. . . . He is interested in teaching high school math, but he is uncertified and has commitments to the community college on Tuesdays and Thursdays. He admits he is a bit worried about classroom management with high schoolers.

Finding a model that accommodates both Ms. Adams and Mr. Harris, while taking advantage of their complementary strengths, seems like the most obvious thing in the world. For readers who wonder why such changes are even classified as a reform rather than an overdue adjustment, we're right there with you.

For all the distractions, remembering the human aspects of education is crucial to securing lasting change that benefits students, teachers, and parents. And as Corey Mohn reminds us, the focus on human beings can build enthusiasm that blossoms into broader movements. When these movements spring up—whether around workforce education or otherwise—they need to keep the progress of individuals at their center and not get distracted by sloganeering or lofty promises detached from the individual work itself. The Center for Advanced Professional Studies (CAPS) Network makes sure to identify the needs—and motivations—of the students doing the work themselves and harnesses those needs in building a broader movement. In a revealing illustration, Mohn offers a snapshot of how CAPS students went about prototyping a new concept, initially known as the Hug Chair, designed to help comfort children with autism. Corey writes:

Utilizing existing pump technology and rudimentary building skills, they constructed a piece of furniture . . . [that] could be the prototype for a commercial product. Suddenly the engineering students were pulling in business students ("We need market research. How much would a therapist or parent pay for this?"), medicine students ("What else do we need to know about autism as we finalize the design?"), and education students ("How do we build a chair that will fit appropriately in a classroom and not be a distraction?"). Eventually, the Sensory Chair emerged as a final product, received an Edison Award (the first time students had ever won one of these prestigious prizes), and was acquired and licensed internationally.

With that enthusiasm and excitement in place, Corey says that the key ingredients in movement building are identifying the people who share your purpose and being curious enough to learn from them and altruistic enough to support them. In other words, being successful does not require shouting about your work and marching forward. It's about helping the human beings in the movement make progress together.

Indeed, as Beth illuminates, even personalization efforts revolve around creating time for more and deeper interactions between educators and students, not just throwing technology in a building for its own sake.

Turn to Policy Only When There's No Other Way

We think the chapters make clear that reinvention is mainly driven by a diligent, deliberate, two-steps-forward-one-step-back commitment to practice. It's much more a matter of doing and learning than of sweeping policy change. Equally clear, however, is that there are times when policy eventually looms as an insurmountable obstacle—and changing laws or regulations becomes essential. Joel Rose documents how the School of One grew into the pretty successful New Classrooms model but also how the promise of such efforts is ultimately limited by existing state assessment systems and staffing rules. The kinds of microschools that Michael McShane describes are already flourishing, but their scalability and quality also depend on state laws governing education choice, licensure, and finance.

So, yes, for the policy wonks reading this, there are a few things that clearly need to be addressed. From these chapters, it's clear that policymakers should reconsider current, outdated practices—step-and-lane pay scales, advancement through school based on seat time, siloed classrooms—and expand the notion of what a school can look like. We should enable schools to move away from one-size-fits-all factory-model routines, whether by expanding options, reducing licensure barriers, making assessment more agile, or removing bureaucratic hurdles for schools and districts. And we should reexamine how procurement creates obstacles to rethinking curriculum and instruction.

But there's also some advice for our fellow analysts and thought leaders who spend a lot of time thinking about policy. While those on the ground are working with urgency, failing, iterating, and trying again, our job isn't necessarily to make headlines about the winners and losers. Instead, we should help make the jobs of practitioners easier so they are more likely to succeed.

There's a tendency to approach education reinvention as a crusade. This can lead to a lot of rhetoric that seems more focused on drawing political lines than bringing viable solutions to the surface. The striking thing is that if we can temper the rhetoric and gain a little perspective, it's quickly apparent that so many of the routines that hamper students and frustrate parents also make life tough for teachers. When we look at assessments or mastery learning, the fact that so many students are stuck, at any given moment, tackling tasks that are either too demanding or not demanding enough is a huge problem. It's bad for learning and engagement alike. This is less about good guys versus bad guys and more about problem-solving. When reformers or policymakers start with the assumptions and rhetoric of conflict, the adrenaline rush can lead them to lose the plot. Instead, let's focus on shared pain and problems—and then search for the solutions that solve those problems. All too often we lead with our talking points or solutions rather than making sure we're all on the same page about what we're trying to solve.

As a result, we should focus more on process. Are the rethinkers and reinventors learning the right lessons as they implement? Are they appropriately adapting to changing technologies and other conditions? And can we consider the efforts to rethink learning through the lens of its impact on stakeholders—students, teachers, and parents—rather than its alignment to an ideology or favored grand plan?

PARTING THOUGHTS

We tackled this book because we've spent a lot of time in conversations devoted to the urgency and inevitability of educational reinvention. Those discussions tend to feature all manner of well-meaning advocates, funders, experts, and policymakers. Too rarely, though, do they feature the voices of those leading this work. While this is understandable, given that those doing the work are busy, well, *doing* the work, it can have unfortunate consequences for our understanding of what happens when rubber meets road.

This volume represents one small effort to address that gap. It brings to the surface both how hard this work can be and how there are promising solutions. Those solutions all start with solving a problem. They pay attention to the human parts of this work—helping people shift their mindsets, not just their routines. They don't just focus on the newfangled thing or get excited about technology for its own sake. They ground those things in the problem they're trying to solve or the goal they're trying to achieve. And they recognize that while there were once well-thought-out reasons for the routines we have today in schools, the context around those routines has changed—which means it's time to rethink the routines as well. That's a view that focuses not on blaming people but on rolling up our sleeves and getting to work together. That isn't sexy stuff. But it's the actual work that makes a tangible difference.

Notes

Introduction

1. "Enrollment Tracker: 2020–2022," Return2LearnTracker, https://www.returntolearntracker.net/2020-22-enrollment-changes/.

2. Adam Newman, Nicholas Java, and Ria Bharadwaj, "School Disrupted: Investigating K–12 District Public School Enrollment Trends," *Tyton Partners* blog, October 11, 2022, https://tytonpartners.com/school-disrupted-investigating-k-12-district-public-school-enrollment-trends/.

3. Peter Jamison et al., "Home Schooling's Rise from Fringe to Fastest-Growing Form of Education," *Washington Post*, October 31, 2023, https://www.washingtonpost.com/education/interactive/2023/homeschooling-growth-data-by-district/.

4. "ICYMI: Florida Ranked #1 in Nation for Parent Involvement in Education," Florida Department of Education, December 12, 2022, https://www.fldoe.org/newsroom/latest-news/icymi-florida-ranked-1-in-nation-for-parent-involvement-in-education.

5. John Kristof, Drew Catt, and Colyn Ritter, "Educational Choice's Blurred (Political) Lines," *Engage by EdChoice*, March 28, 2022, https://www.edchoice.org/engage/educational-choices-blurred-political-lines/.

6. Madeline Will, "Teachers Are Stressed and Disrespected, but Happier Than Last Year: 7 Takeaways from New Poll," *Education Week*, May 22, 2023, https://www.edweek.org/teaching-learning/teachers-are-stressed-and-disrespected-but-happier-than-last-year-7-takeaways-from-new-poll/2023/05.

7. Sy Doan et al., *Teacher Well-Being and Intentions to Leave: Findings from the 2023 State of the American Teacher Survey* (Santa Monica, CA: RAND Corporation, June 2023), https://www.rand.org/pubs/research_reports/RRA1108-8.html.

8. *American Microschools: A Sector Analysis* (Las Vegas: National Microschooling Center, April 2023), https://microschoolingcenter.org/hubfs/American%20Microschools%2C%20A%20Sector%20Analysis%202023.pdf.

9. "New Data Show How the Pandemic Affected Learning Across Whole Communities," Harvard Graduate School of Education, May 11, 2023, https://www.gse.harvard.edu/ideas/news/23/05/new-data-show-how-pandemic-affected-learning-across-whole-communities.

10. Evie Blad, "Educators See Gaps in Kids' Emotional Growth Due to Pandemic," *Education Week*, February 24, 2022, https://www.edweek.org/leadership/educators-see-gaps-in-kids-emotional-growth-due-to-pandemic/2022/02.

11. "Education Next Survey of Public Opinion: Trends Through 2022," *Education Next*, last updated August 16, 2022, https://www.educationnext.org/ednext-poll-interactive-trends-through-2022-public-opinion/.

12. Michael B. Horn, *From Reopen to Reinvent: (Re)Creating School for Every Child* (Hoboken, NJ: Jossey-Bass, 2022).

13. Frederick M. Hess, *The Great School Rethink* (Cambridge, MA: Harvard Education Press, 2023).
14. For information about this initiative, see https://bellwether.org/beta/assembly/.
15. David Tyack and Larry Cuban, *Tinkering Toward Utopia: A Century of Public School Reform* (Cambridge, MA: Harvard University Press, 1995), 40–41.
16. Frederick M. Hess, *Spinning Wheels: The Politics of Urban School Reform* (Washington, DC: Brookings Institution Press, 1998).

Chapter 1

1. Large language models are artificial intelligence systems designed to understand and generate human language text. These models are typically trained on vast (hence "large") amounts of text data from the internet and other sources, allowing them to acquire a deep understanding of language patterns, semantics, and grammar.
2. Generative AI refers to artificial intelligence systems that can create new data or content, such as text, images, music, or videos. These systems can produce novel and creative output by learning patterns from existing data.
3. "Gartner Hype Cycle," Gartner, https://www.gartner.com/en/research/methodologies /gartner-hype-cycle.
4. Kevin Mahnken, "NAEP Scores 'Flashing Red' After a Lost Generation of Learning for 13-Year-Olds," *The 74*, June 21, 2023, https://www.the74million.org/article/naep-scores -flashing-red-after-a-lost-generation-of-learning-for-13-year-olds/.
5. *First Annual Merrimack College Teacher Survey: 2022 Results* (North Andover, MA: Merrimack College and EdWeek Research Center, 2022), https://www.edweek.org/products /todays-teachers-are-deeply-disillusioned-survey-data-confirms.
6. Arthur Jones II, "Most of the US Is Dealing with a Teaching Shortage, but the Data Isn't So Simple," ABC News, February 11, 2023, https://abcnews.go.com/US/map-shows-us-states -dealing-teaching-shortage-data/story?id=96752632.
7. Gerard Robinson, "America Is Facing a Shortage of STEM Teachers: Here's One Way to Solve It," *The 74*, October 13, 2023, https://www.the74million.org/article/a-solution-to -americas-k-12-stem-teacher-shortage-endowed-chairs/.
8. Wenting Ma et al., "Intelligent Tutoring Systems and Learning Outcomes: A Meta-Analysis," *Journal of Educational Psychology* 106, no. 4 (2014): 901–18, doi: 10.1037/a0037123.
9. Kenneth R. Koedinger et al., "An Astonishing Regularity in Student Learning Rate," *Proceedings of the National Academy of Sciences of the United States of America* 120, no. 13 (March 20, 2023): doi: 10.1073/pnas.2221311120.
10. GPTs are a class of large language models. They are "pretrained" by being exposed to vast amounts of text data from the internet and are then fine-tuned on specific tasks. GPT models can generate human-like text, answer questions, translate languages, and perform various other language-related tasks.
11. Richard E. Mayer, "Using Multimedia for E-Learning," *Journal of Computer Assisted Learning* 33, no. 5 (June 13, 2017): 403–23, doi: 10.1111/jcal.12197.
12. Justin Reich, *Failure to Disrupt: Why Technology Alone Can't Transform Education* (Cambridge, MA: Harvard University Press, 2020).
13. "NCTE Position Statement on Machine Scoring," National Council of Teachers of English, April 20, 2013, https://ncte.org/statement/machine_scoring/.
14. Semire Dikli, "An Overview of Automated Scoring of Essays," *Journal of Technology, Learning, and Assessment* 5, no. 1 (August 2006), https://files.eric.ed.gov/fulltext/EJ843855.pdf.

15. *Elevating Math Scores: The Ongoing Success of MAP Accelerator* (Mountain View, CA: Khan Academy, 2022), https://blog.khanacademy.org/wp-content/uploads/2023/09/MAP_Accelerator_21_22_Brief-1.pdf.

16. "Digital Divide," Education GPS, https://gpseducation.oecd.org/revieweducationpolicies/#!node=41748&filter=all.

17. Michael Trucano, "AI and the Next Digital Divide in Education," Brookings Institution, July 10, 2023, https://www.brookings.edu/articles/ai-and-the-next-digital-divide-in-education/.

18. *The Ethical Framework for AI in Education* (Buckingham, UK: Institute for Ethical AI in Education, 2021), https://www.buckingham.ac.uk/wp-content/uploads/2021/03/The-Institute-for-Ethical-AI-in-Education-The-Ethical-Framework-for-AI-in-Education.pdf.

19. National Institute of Standards and Technology, *Artificial Intelligence Risk Management Framework*, AI RMF 1.0 (Washington, DC: US Department of Commerce, January 2023), https://nvlpubs.nist.gov/nistpubs/ai/NIST.AI.100-1.pdf.

20. Debora L. Roorda et al., "The Influence of Affective Teacher–Student Relationships on Students' School Engagement and Achievement: A Meta-Analytic Approach," *Review of Educational Research* 81, no. 4 (December 2011): 493–529, doi: 10.3102/0034654311421793.

Chapter 3

1. For the purposes of this chapter, I'm using the term *system* to refer to a group of interacting or interrelated elements that act according to a set of rules to form a unified whole. In the context of K–12, I acknowledge that systems exist at multiple levels—the classroom, the school, local and state agencies, and the overarching national structure—and that opportunities and levers for personalization vary and interact. However, from the learner standpoint, all of these systems have relevance and are basically experienced as one.

2. Tim Hodges, "School Engagement Is More Than Just Talk," Gallup, October 25, 2018, https://www.gallup.com/education/244022/school-engagement-talk.aspx; Linda Jacobson, "Exclusive Data: Thousands of Schools at Risk of Closing Due to Enrollment Loss," *The 74*, January 9, 2024, https://www.the74million.org/article/exclusive-data-thousands-of-schools-at-risk-of-closing-due-to-enrollment-loss/.

3. Interested readers can access these on TLA's website, https://learningaccelerator.org/.

4. Christina Quattrocchi, "How Lindsay Unified Redesigned Itself from the Ground Up," *EdSurge*, June 17, 2014, https://www.edsurge.com/news/2014-06-17-how-lindsay-unified-redesigned-itself-from-the-ground-up.

5. This term is taken from construction, but its metaphorical usage in education comes from Bea McGarvey, who uses the term "weight-bearing" walls in her work in Mass Customized Learning.

6. Dan Meyer, "The Misunderstanding About Education That Cost Mark Zuckerberg $100 Million," *Mathworlds* (Substack), October 11, 2023, https://danmeyer.substack.com/p/the-misunderstanding-about-education.

7. Nithi Thomas and Beth Rabbitt, *Innovative Learning Implementation Framework: A Guide to Shifting System Conditions for Success and Scale* (Princeton, NJ: The Learning Accelerator, 2019), https://bplawassets.learningaccelerator.org/artifacts/pdf_files/Innovative-Learning-Implementation-Framework-TLA.pdf.

8. David Dockterman, "Insights from 200+ Years of Personalized Learning," *npj Science of Learning* 3, no. 15 (September 2018), doi: 10.1038/s41539-018-0033-x.

9. Jack Schneider and Ethan Hutt, "Making the Grade: A History of the A–F Marking Scheme," *Journal of Curriculum Studies* 46, no. 2 (2014): 201–24, doi: 10.1080/00220272.2013.790480.

10. Russell L. Ackoff, "Systems Thinking and Thinking Systems," *System Dynamics Review* 10, no. 2–3 (Summer–Autumn 1994): 175–88, doi: 10.1002/sdr.4260100206.

Chapter 4

1. For more on declining enrollment, see *Trends in Enrollment in US Teacher Preparation Programs: 2009–2021*, Research Brief 2023-6 (University Park, PA: Penn State Center for Education Evaluation and Policy Analysis, May 2023), https://ceepablog.files.wordpress .com/2023/08/trends-in-enrollment-in-us-tpp-enrollment-penn-state-ceepa-may-2023 -final.pdf; for more on parents recommending the teaching profession, see "The 54th Annual PDK Poll," PDK Poll, https://pdkpoll.org/2022-pdk-poll-results/.
2. Larry Cuban, "Whatever Happened to Team Teaching?" *Larry Cuban on School Reform and Classroom Practice*, December 9, 2018, https://larrycuban.wordpress.com/2018/12/09 /whatever-happened-to-team-teaching/.
3. Richard Lennon Audrain, "Looking Backward, Inward, and Forward: The Genealogy of, and Conceptual and Empirical Evidence for, the Next Education Workforce" (PhD diss., Arizona State University, 2023), https://keep.lib.asu.edu/taxonomy/term/154390.
4. "School Reform Autopsy," *New York Times*, February 19, 1973, https://www.nytimes.com /1973/02/19/archives/school-reform-autopsy.html.
5. The Coalition to Reimagine the Teaching Role, founded in 2021, works to create the conditions where all K–12 educators thrive in collaborative and sustainable roles so that all students realize their unique potential. In 2024, more than thirty-five organizations belong to the coalition, with members ranging from nonprofits that support schools designing new staffing models to higher education institutions to the national teacher unions. For more information, see https://teachingrolereimagined.org.
6. "Elements of the Next Education Workforce," Next Education Workforce, https://workforce .education.asu.edu/resource/elements-of-the-next-education-workforce.
7. "Research Shows Results," Opportunity Culture, https://www.opportunityculture.org /research/.
8. "District Directory Information, Mesa Unified District," National Center for Education Statistics, https://nces.ed.gov/ccd/districtsearch/district_detail.asp?ID2=0404970.
9. "Results from the Year One Survey of Next Education Workforce Teachers," Next Education Workforce, https://workforce.education.asu.edu/resource/results-from-the-year-one -survey-of-next-education-workforce-teachers.
10. *Here Today, Gone Tomorrow?: What America Must Do to Attract and Retain the Educators and School Staff Our Students Need*, Report from the AFT Teacher and School Staff Shortage Task Force (Washington, DC: American Federation of Teachers, July 2022), https://www.aft .org/sites/default/files/media/2022/taskforcereport0722.pdf.
11. "Creating Shared and Flexible Learning Spaces: A Continuum for Rethinking Space," Next Education Workforce, https://workforce.education.asu.edu/resource/creating-shared-and -flexible-learning-spaces-a-continuum-for-rethinking-space.
12. A set of solutions to create financially sustainable strategic school staffing models that we created in partnership with Education Resource Strategies can be found at "Sustainable Financial Models," Next Education Workforce, https://workforce.education.asu.edu/collection /sustainable-financial-models.

Chapter 5

1. See Todd Rose, *The End of Average: How We Succeed in a World That Values Sameness* (New York: HarperOne, 2016) and Frederick Hess, *The Same Thing Over and Over: How*

School Reformers Get Stuck in Yesterday's Ideas (Cambridge, MA: Harvard University Press, 2010).

2. As cited in William H. Jeynes, *American Educational History: School, Society, and the Common Good* (Thousand Oaks, CA: Sage Publications, 2007), 145.

3. Among the many books on the subject, see especially Rose, *The End of Average* and Hess, *The Same Thing Over and Over*.

4. Rose, *The End of Average*, Kindle edition.

5. Rose, *The End of Average*.

6. "Household Pulse Survey: Measuring Emergent Social and Economic Matters Facing U.S. Households," updated April 2, 2024, United States Census Bureau, https://www.census.gov/data/experimental-data-products/household-pulse-survey.html; Peter Jamison et al., "Home Schooling's Rise from Fringe to Fastest-Growing Form of Education," *Washington Post*, October 31, 2023, https://www.washingtonpost.com/education/interactive/2023/homeschooling-growth-data-by-district/; Thomas S. Dee, "Where the Kids Went: Nonpublic Schooling and Demographic Change During the Pandemic Exodus from Public Schools," Urban Institute, February 9, 2023, https://www.urban.org/research/publication/where-kids-went-nonpublic-schooling-and-demographic-change-during-pandemic.

7. Jamison et al., "Home Schooling's Rise from Fringe."

8. William Brangham and Mary Fecteau, "How Homeschooling's Rise During the Pandemic Has Impacted Traditional School Enrollment," *PBS News Hour*, May 18, 2023, https://www.pbs.org/newshour/show/how-homeschoolings-rise-during-the-pandemic-has-impacted-traditional-school-enrollment; Athena Jones and Nicquel Terry Ellis, "'A Form of Resistance': More Black Families are Choosing to Homeschool Their Children," CNN, March 1, 2023, https://www.cnn.com/2023/03/01/us/black-families-home-school-reaj/index.html; Carolyn Thompson, "Homeschooling Surge Continues Despite Schools Reopening," Associated Press, April 14, 2022, https://apnews.com/article/covid-business-health-buffalo-education-d37f4f1d12e57b72e5ddf67d4f897d9a; "Homeschooling," *Last Week Tonight with John Oliver*, October 8, 2023, https://www.hbo.com/last-week-tonight-with-john-oliver/season-10/12-october-8-2023-homeschooling.

9. *Populace Insights: Purpose of Education Index* (Burlington, MA: Populace, 2022), https://static1.squarespace.com/static/59153bc0e6f2e109b2a85cbc/t/63e96b44a0e46d79a10ecf26/1676241761790/Purpose+of+Education+Index.pdf.

10. *Choose to Learn: Connecting In- and Out-of-School Learning in a Post-Pandemic World* (New York: Tyton Partners, 2022), https://4213961.fs1.hubspotusercontent-na1.net/hubfs/4213961/Tyton%20Partners%20Choose%20to%20Learn%202022%20Connecting%20in-%20and%20out-of-school%20learning%20in%20a%20post-pandemic%20world.pdf.

11. Lydia Saad, "Historically Low Faith in U.S. Institutions Continues," *Gallup News*, July 6, 2023, https://news.gallup.com/poll/508169/historically-low-faith-institutions-continues.aspx.

12. Frederick M. Hess, "Democrats Have Lost Public Confidence on Education, but the GOP Hasn't Gained It," American Enterprise Institute, April 2022, https://www.aei.org/wp-content/uploads/2022/04/Democrats-Have-Lost-Public-Confidence-on-Education.pdf.

13. Kevin Mahnken, "Rash of New Polls Raises Red Flags for Democrats on Education," *The 74*, July 20, 2022, https://www.the74million.org/article/rash-of-new-polls-raise-red-flags-for-democrats-on-education/.

14. Hess, "Democrats Have Lost Public Confidence."

15. Jay P. Greene and James D. Paul, *Does School Choice Need Bipartisan Support?: An Empirical Analysis of the Legislative Record* (Washington, DC: American Enterprise Institute, September 2021), https://www.aei.org/wp-content/uploads/2021/09/Does-School-Choice-Need -Bipartisan-Support.pdf.

16. Colyn Ritter, "2024 EdChoice Share: Exploring Where America's Students Are Educated," Engage by EdChoice, January 17, 2024, https://www.edchoice.org/engage/2024-edchoice -share-exploring-where-americas-students-are-educated/.

17. Milton Friedman, *Capitalism and Freedom* (Chicago: University of Chicago Press, 1962).

18. "School Choice Facts & Statistics," EdChoice, last modified April 17, 2023, https://www .edchoice.org/school-choice/fast-facts/.

19. Marc LeBlond and Ed Tarnowski, "Educational Freedom and Choice Hits Escape Velocity: End-of-Session Wrap-Up," Engage by EdChoice, July 19, 2023, https://www.edchoice.org /engage/educational-freedom-and-choice-hits-escape-velocity-end-of-session-wrap/.

20. Amber Raub, "Florida Sees Record Number of Students Receiving School Voucher Funding," CBS12, August 21, 2023, https://cbs12.com/news/local/governor-ron-desantis -school-voucher-funding-record-number-students-receiving-applications-funds-step-up -for-students-palm-beach-martin-st-lucie-indian-river-okeechobee-county-schools-florida -august-21-2023.

21. Philip Suderman, "Micro School Entrepreneur Struggles to Make Sense of Zoning," Institute for Justice, August 17, 2023, https://ij.org/press-release/micro-school-entrepreneur -struggles-to-make-sense-of-zoning/.

22. Kerry McDonald, "Why Can't a Retired U.S. Navy Officer and Engineer Open a Private School in Nevada?" *Forbes*, February 22, 2023, https://www.forbes.com/sites/kerry mcdonald/2023/02/22/why-cant-a-retired-us-navy-officer-and-engineer-open-a-private -school-in-nevada/.

23. Linda Jacobson, "'Growing Pains': Microschools Face Regulatory Maze as Approach Takes Hold," *The 74*, September 21, 2023, https://www.the74million.org/article/growing-pains -microschools-face-regulatory-maze-as-approach-takes-hold/.

24. "SB 166: Legalize Microschools," Libertas Institute, https://libertas.org/bill/sb-166-legalize -microschools/; "Microschools Face Major Problems," Libertas Institute, https://libertas.org /op-eds/microschools-face-major-problems/.

25. "Diffusion of Innovation Theory," Behavioral Change Models, https://sphweb.bumc.bu.edu /otlt/mph-modules/sb/behavioralchangetheories/behavioralchangetheories4.html.

Chapter 6

1. Larry Cooley, Maud Seghers, and Jenny Perlman Robinson, "Planning for Scale: The Education Scalability Checklist," Brookings Institution, February 24, 2021, https://www.brookings .edu/articles/planning-for-scale-the-education-scalability-checklist/.

2. *Supporting Students: Investing in Innovation and Quality*, College-Ready Work Monographs (Seattle: Bill & Melinda Gates Foundation, 2011), https://docs.gatesfoundation.org /documents/supporting-students.pdf.

3. "Education," Walton Family Foundation, https://www.waltonfamilyfoundation.org/our -work/education-program.

4. LaVerne Evans Srinivasan, "What Changes to the U.S. Education System Are Needed to Support Long-Term Success for All Americans?" *Carnegie Reporter*, May 10, 2021, https:// www.carnegie.org/our-work/article/what-changes-us-education-system-are-needed -support-long-term-success-all-americans/.

5. "Charter Schools Program," US Department of Education Office of Elementary & Secondary Education, https://oese.ed.gov/offices/office-of-discretionary-grants-support-services/charter-schools-program.

6. Peter Jamison et al., "Home Schooling's Rise from Fringe to Fastest-Growing Form of Education," *Washington Post*, October 31, 2023, https://www.washingtonpost.com/education/interactive/2023/homeschooling-growth-data-by-district/.

7. Albert Cheng and Daniel Hamlin, "Contemporary Homeschooling Arrangements: An Analysis of Three Waves of Nationally Representative Data," *Educational Policy* 37, no. 5 (July 2023): 1444–66, doi: 10.1177/08959048221103795.

8. *The Public, Parents, and K–12 Education: A National Polling Report, July 2023* (Washington, DC: Morning Consult and EdChoice, July 2023), https://edchoice.morningconsult intelligence.com/assets/270294.pdf.

9. John Kristof, Colyn Ritter, and Paul DiPerna, *2023 Schooling in America: What Do the Public and Parents Say About K–12 Education?* (Indianapolis: EdChoice, August 2023), https://www.edchoice.org/wp-content/uploads/2023/07/SIA-2023-REPORT-FINAL.pdf.

10. *The Public, Parents, and K–12 Education: A National Polling Report, October 2023* (Washington, DC: Morning Consult and EdChoice, October 2023), https://edchoice.morningconsult intelligence.com/assets/270357.pdf.

11. Edward E. Gordon and Elaine H. Gordon, *Centuries of Tutoring: A History of Alternative Education in America and Western Europe* (Lanham, MD: University Press of America, 1990).

12. Quentin Letts, "Everything You Need to Know About Tory MP Rory Stewart," *Tatler*, October 8, 2019, https://www.tatler.com/article/everything-you-need-to-know-about-rory-stewart-mp.

13. George H. Copa and Virginia H. Pease, "The Comprehensive High School: An Historical Perspective" (working paper, National Center for Research in Vocational Education, Berkeley, CA, 1992), https://files.eric.ed.gov/fulltext/ED352520.pdf.

14. David Strang, "The Administrative Transformation of American Education: School District Consolidation, 1938–1980," *Administrative Science Quarterly* 32, no. 3 (September 1987): 352–66, doi: 10.2307/2392909.

15. Claudia Goldin, "The Human Capital Century," *Education Next* 3, no. 1 (Winter 2003, updated July 2006), https://www.educationnext.org/the-human-capital-century/.

16. Cheryl V. Jackson, "Carmel High School Seems to Have It All and TikTok Users Are Finding Out in Viral Videos," *Indianapolis Star*, February 13, 2023, https://eu.indystar.com/story/news/local/hamilton-county/carmel/2023/02/13/carmel-high-school-students-tiktok-videos-natatorium-stadium-auditorium-studios-auto-shop/69899563007/.

17. John Dewey, *The School and Society: Being Three Lectures* (Chicago: University of Chicago Press, 1907), 19.

18. *The Public, Parents, and K–12 Education, October 2023*.

19. Jay P. Greene, "Buckets into the Sea," in *With the Best of Intentions: How Philanthropy is Reshaping K–12 Education*, ed. Frederick M. Hess (Cambridge, MA: Harvard Education Press, 2005), 71–72.

20. Greene, "Buckets into the Sea."

21. Greene, "Buckets into the Sea."

22. For the purpose of full disclosure, my research has been supported by the VELA fund.

23. Kynala Phillips, "How Much Do Kansas City Area School Districts Pay New Teachers? Here's the Data," *Kansas City Star*, updated September 6, 2022, https://www.kansascity.com/news/local/education/article264579111.html.

24. *Opposition Report: Pandemic Pods* (Washington, DC: National Education Association and Center for Enterprise Strategy, 2020), https://www.wsj.com/public/resources/documents /Prenda.pdf.

Chapter 7
1. For more information about the project, see https://bvcaps.wixsite.com/sensorydesign.
2. Tom Vander Ark, "How the CAPS Network is Transforming Career Readiness," *Forbes*, Feb 25, 2022, https://www.forbes.com/sites/tomvanderark/2022/02/24/how-the-caps-network -is-transforming-career-readiness/.
3. "Alumni Impact," CAPS Network, https://yourcapsnetwork.org/alumni/.

Chapter 8
1. Beth Hawkins, "New Research Predicts Steep COVID Learning Losses Will Widen Already Dramatic Achievement Gaps Within Classrooms," *The 74*, June 9, 2020, https://www.the 74million.org/article/new-research-predicts-steep-covid-learning-losses-will-widen-already -dramatic-achievement-gaps-within-classrooms/.
2. Karyn Lewis et al., *The Widening Achievement Divide During COVID-19,* NWEA Research Brief (Portland, OR: Center for School and Student Progress, NWEA, November 2022), https://www.nwea.org/uploads/2022/11/CSSP-Brief_Widening-achievement-divide-COV ID-19.pdf.
3. "NAEP Data Explorer," National Assessment of Education Progress (NAEP), https://www .nationsreportcard.gov/ndecore/landing.
4. Lou Ann Sears, "Edward Lee Thorndike (1874–1949): A Look at His Contributions to Learning and Reading," in *Shaping the Reading Field: The Impact of Early Reading Pioneers, Scientific Research, and Progressive Ideas*, ed. Susan E. Israel and E. Jennifer Monaghan (Newark, DE: International Reading Association, 2007): 119–39, https://www.readinghall offame.org/sites/default/files/deceased_member_files/a_look_at_his_contributions_to _learning_and_reading.pdf.
5. Zuowei Wang et al., "Decoding and Reading Comprehension: A Test of the Decoding Threshold Hypothesis," *Journal of Educational Psychology* 111, no. 3 (2019): 387–401, doi: 10.1037/edu0000302.
6. The full concept map can be found at https://teachtoone.org/mapping-middle-school -math/.
7. Sarah Mervosh and Ashley Wu, "Math Scores Fell in Nearly Every State, and Reading Dipped on National Exam," *New York Times*, October 24, 2022, https://www.nytime s.com/2022/10/24/us/math-reading-scores-pandemic.html.
8. Richard Elmore, "Improving the Instructional Core" (draft paper, Harvard University Graduate School of Education, 2008), https://teacher.justinwells.net/Downloads/improving _the_instructional_core_elmore_2008.pdf.
9. "The 50 Best Inventions of 2009," *TIME*, November 12, 2009, https://content.time.com /time/specials/packages/article/0,28804,1934027_1934003_1933977,00.html.
10. Jesse Margolis, *Three-Year MAP Growth at Schools Using Teach to One: Math* (New York: MarGrady Research, February 2019), http://margrady.com/tto/.
11. Margaret Raymond, "The Terrible Truth: Current Solutions to COVID Learning Loss Are Doomed to Fail," *The 74*, April 24, 2023, https://www.the74million.org/article/the-terrible -truth-current-solutions-to-covid-learning-loss-are-doomed-to-fail/.

12. In 2022–23, students using Roadmaps as a supplemental program learned, on average, 1.4 skills per active week. This number added to the total number of skills they learned in their core program yields their total pace.

13. John Sweller, Jeroen J. G. van Merrienboer, and Fred G. W. C. Paas, "Cognitive Architecture and Instructional Design," *Educational Psychology Review* 10, no. 3 (September 1998): 251–96, doi: 10.1023/a:1022193728205.

14. Sweller, van Merrienboer, and Paas, "Cognitive Architecture."

15. Dan Willingham, "When and How Neuroscience Applies to Education," *Phi Delta Kappan* 89, no. 6 (February 2008): 421–23, doi: 10.1177/003172170808900607.

16. "Building Blocks for Learning," Center for Whole-Child Education, https://turnaroundusa .org/what-we-do/tools/building-blocks/.

17. Ricarda Steinmayr et al., "The Importance of Students' Motivation for Their Academic Achievement—Replicating and Extending Previous Findings," *Frontiers in Psychology* 10 (July 2019), doi: 10.3389/fpsyg.2019.01730.

18. Kevin Mahnken, "Study: Chicago Tutoring Program Delivered Huge Math Gains; Personalization May Be the Key," *The 74*, March 8, 2021, https://www.the74million.org /study-chicago-tutoring-program-delivered-huge-math-gains-personalization-may-be -the-key/.

19. *The Opportunity Myth* (New York: TNTP, 2018), https://tntp.org/wp-content/uploads /2023/02/TNTP_The-Opportunity-Myth_Web.pdf.

20. Sarah Schwartz, "California Adopts Controversial New Math Framework. Here's What's in It," *Education Week*, July 12, 2023, https://www.edweek.org/teaching-learning/california -adopts-controversial-new-math-framework-heres-whats-in-it/2023/07.

21. "Independent Study Confirms Teach to One Roadmaps Provides Students with a Pathway to Proficiency on State Math Assessments," New Classrooms, April 8, 2024, https://new classrooms.org/2024/04/08/independent-study-confirms-teach-to-one-roadmaps-provides -students-with-a-pathway-to-proficiency-on-state-math-assessments/

22. In a PCBL supplemental offering that uses multiyear progressions, students would still be able to access sixth- and seventh-grade skills as part of their core math program.

Chapter 9

1. *Measuring Forward: Emerging Trends in K–12 Assessment Innovation* (Aurora Institute, Center for Assessment, Center for Innovation in Education, Envision Learning Partners, Great Schools Partnership, and KnowledgeWorks, 2021), https://knowledgeworks.org/wp -content/uploads/2021/11/assessment-innovation-state-trends.pdf.

2. Carl Kaestle, *Testing Policy in the United States: A Historical Perspective* (Princeton, NJ: Educational Testing Service, Gordon Commission on the Future of Assessment in Education, 2013), https://www.ets.org/Media/Research/pdf/kaestle_testing_policy_us_historical _perspective.pdf.

3. James W. Pellegrino, Naomi Chudowsky, and Robert Glaser, eds., *Knowing What Students Know: The Science and Design of Educational Assessment* (Washington, DC: National Academy Press, 2001): 41, doi: 10.17226/10019.

4. Martin R. West, Beth A. Morton, and Corinne M. Herlihy, "Achievement Network's Investing in Innovation Expansion: Impacts on Educator Practice and Student Achievement" (research paper, Center for Education Policy Research, Harvard University, 2016), https:// cepr.harvard.edu/files/cepr/files/anet-research-report.pdf.

5. Walter Kintsch and Teun A. van Dijk, "Toward a Model of Text Comprehension and Production," *Psychological Review* 85, no. 5 (September 1978): 363–94, doi: 10.1037/0033
-295X.85.5.363.

6. Reid Smith et al., "The Role of Background Knowledge in Reading Comprehension: A
Critical Review," *Reading Psychology* 42, no. 3 (February 2021), doi: 10.1080/02702711
.2021.1888348.

Chapter 10

1. Steven Levy, "'Hackers' and 'Information Wants to Be Free,'" *Medium*, Nov 21, 2014,
https://medium.com/backchannel/the-definitive-story-of-information-wants-to-be-free
-a8d95427641c#.y7d0amvr3.

Acknowledgments

Frederick M. Hess, Michael B. Horn,
and Juliet Squire

This book grew out of overlapping work that the three of us had been conducting over several years. We have all long been fascinated by efforts to rethink and reinvent American schooling—and we've tackled that work in an array of books, podcasts, white papers, advisory and consulting projects, and more. As we were comparing notes in 2023, we found ourselves discussing the constraints inherent in the way we could write and talk about this work. The big issue? We come at all of this as talkers, writers, and consultants rather than doers, which means we tend to focus on broad strokes, conceptual models, and illustrative examples rather than the practical complexities and hard-earned lessons that practitioners work through on a daily basis. We agreed it would be valuable for those actually doing this work to share first-person insights about the relevant opportunities and challenges.

One of the reasons we so rarely read careful, reflective appraisals by those doing this work is . . . they're busy doing the work. So, first and foremost, thank you to the contributors who found time—frequently during their evenings, weekends, and holidays—to craft and revise these remarkable windows into the world of K–12 rethinking. We're indebted to them for their hard work, honesty, and genial collaboration.

Thank you as well to the terrific team at Harvard Education Press, who helped shepherd this volume from the beginning stages through the finish line. We'd also like to thank Greg Fournier, who provided crucial coordination, invaluable editorial feedback, and sleeves-up collaboration through the course of this project. We'd also like to thank Greg's able colleague Anna Coulter for her assistance.

Rick would like to offer special thanks to the American Enterprise Institute, the place that has provided him a vibrant and supportive home for more than two decades, and to its president, Robert Doar.

Michael extends a thank you to all those who have collaborated with him in the explorations of rethinking and reinventing over the past few years, including Diane Tavenner, Anthony Kim, Jeff Wetzler, Aylon Samouha, Thomas Arnett, Julia Freeland Fisher, and the rest of the team at the Clayton Christensen Institute. And a thank you to Michael's wife, Tracy Kim Horn, and their children Madison and Kayla, who constantly push him to reinvent his own thinking.

Julie is grateful to her colleagues at Bellwether who contributed research and insights to the Assembly initiative and helped open the door for this project, including Paul Beach, Kateland Beals, Katrina Boone, Lynne Graziano, Linea Harding, Liz McNamee, Marisa Mission, and Alex Spurrier. She thanks her parents and brother for early words of encouragement and inspiration to work in education, and, above all, she thanks her partner, Justus Myers, for his unending support and for being the first sounding board for every idea, however trivial, grand, or half-formed.

About the Editors and Contributors

EDITORS

Frederick M. Hess is a senior fellow and the director of education policy studies at the American Enterprise Institute (AEI), where he works on K–12 and higher education issues. The author of *Education Week's* popular blog *Rick Hess Straight Up*, Dr. Hess is also an executive editor of *Education Next* and a senior contributor to *Forbes*. He is the founder and chairman of AEI's Conservative Education Reform Network. An educator, political scientist, and author, Dr. Hess has published in popular outlets including the *New York Times*, *USA Today*, the *Wall Street Journal*, and the *Washington Post*. Dr. Hess started his career as a high school social studies teacher and has since taught at colleges including Rice, Harvard, Georgetown, and the University of Virginia. His books include *Spinning Wheels*, *Letters to a Young Education Reformer*, *Cage-Busting Leadership*, *A Search for Common Ground*, *The Great School Rethink*, and *Getting Education Right*. He holds an MA and PhD in government and an MEd in teaching and curriculum from Harvard University.

Michael B. Horn is the cofounder of and a distinguished fellow at the Clayton Christensen Institute for Disruptive Innovation, a nonprofit think tank, and teaches at the Harvard Graduate School of Education. Horn is the author of several books, including *From Reopen to Reinvent*, *Disrupting Class*, *Blended*, *Choosing College*, and *Goodnight Box*, a children's story. He cohosts the top education podcasts *Future U* and *Class Disrupted*. He is a regular contributor to *Forbes* and writes the Substack newsletter *The Future of Education*. Horn also serves as an executive editor at *Education*

Next, and his work has been featured in outlets such as the *New York Times*, the *Washington Post*, *The Atlantic*, *Harvard Business Review*, and NBC. Horn holds a BA in history from Yale University and an MBA from the Harvard Business School.

Juliet Squire is a senior partner in the policy and evaluation practice area at Bellwether. She has been published in outlets such as the *Detroit News*, *U.S. News & World Report*, *Education Next*, *Education Post*, and *The 74*. Before joining Bellwether, Juliet worked at the New Jersey Department of Education, where she oversaw the state's Race to the Top program and developed strategies for advancing technology-driven innovation. Previously, she managed school board relationships and new school development for National Heritage Academies, where she provided support to school leaders, liaised with charter authorizers, and helped to launch new charter schools in Louisiana, New York, and Wisconsin. Juliet began her career at the American Enterprise Institute, where she studied a wide range of issues in K–12 and higher education policy. She is the former board chair of a charter school in Washington, DC. She received her bachelor's degree in political science from Yale University.

CONTRIBUTORS

Sal Khan is the founder and CEO of Khan Academy, a nonprofit with the mission of providing a free, world-class education for anyone, anywhere. He is also the founder of Schoolhouse.world, Khan Lab School, and Khan World School, all nonprofits focused on making world-class, personalized mastery education accessible. Sal's interest in education began while he was an undergraduate at MIT. He developed math software for children with ADHD and tutored fourth- and seventh-grade public school students in Boston. He holds three degrees from MIT and an MBA from Harvard Business School.

Kristen DiCerbo is the chief learning officer at Khan Academy. In this role, she is responsible for driving and communicating the learning strategy for Khan Academy's programs, content, and products to realize deep engagement and better learning outcomes. She leads the content and product management teams, ensuring pedagogical coherence and a research-informed design across Khan Academy's offerings. Prior to coming to Khan Academy, Kristen was the vice president of learning research and design at Pearson. Throughout her career she has focused on conducting and embedding learning science research into digital learning experiences, including work with the Cisco Networking Academy. She also served as a school psychologist in Arizona. Kristen has a BA in psychology and sociology from Hamilton College and an MEd and PhD in educational psychology from Arizona State University.

Rachel Boroditsky is Khan Academy's chief of staff. In this role, Rachel is accountable for driving the strategic planning process; providing strategic and operational support to the CEO, senior leadership team, and board of directors; and supporting special projects. Prior to joining Khan Academy, Rachel was a manager at McKinsey & Company, where she worked with higher education institutions and systems on strategic and operational initiatives, and worked at a literacy and numeracy nonprofit, where she managed the implementation of tablet-based learning programs in Malawi. Rachel has a BA in economics and mathematical methods in the social sciences from Northwestern University.

Scott Ellis is the founder and CEO of MasteryTrack and a national expert in catalyzing blended and mastery learning at scale. Previously, Scott was the founding CEO of The Learning Accelerator and served as the chief strategy officer and chief operating officer of New Teacher Center (NTC). He has also served on the board of trustees for Reading Partners (an education nonprofit that runs reading tutoring programs for children) and the Spondylitis Association of America (a medical nonprofit), and has provided consulting support to dozens of other organizations. In his career before NTC, Scott spent nearly eight years at Hewlett-Packard and managed an internal analytical consulting organization whose role was to help the various HP businesses make better data-driven decisions. Before joining HP, Scott was a consultant at McKinsey & Company. He has an MBA from Stanford and an undergraduate degree in government and economics from Harvard.

Beth Rabbitt is CEO of The Learning Accelerator (TLA). She is a nationally recognized expert in education innovation and blended and personalized learning. Prior to becoming CEO in 2016, Beth was a partner on TLA's start-up team, leading the organization's work to develop educator training systems and research on emerging teaching and learning models and practices. Prior to joining TLA, Beth was a doctoral resident and director of human capital at a start-up school system in Newark, New Jersey, an associate partner at the NewSchools Venture Fund, a consultant to and with Education Resource Strategies, and the founding doctoral fellow at the Harvard Innovation Lab. Beth is a Pahara-Aspen education fellow and serves on the board of several education nonprofits, including Catalyst:Ed and GiveThx. She earned a BA from Dartmouth College and an EdLD from Harvard University, where she was an inaugural cohort member in the University's doctor of education leadership program.

Brent W. Maddin is the executive director of the Next Education Workforce at Arizona State University (ASU). Brent collaborates with colleagues across ASU, preK–12 educators, and the community to redesign models of schooling based on teams of educators with distributed expertise who are better able to deliver on the promise of deeper and personalized learning for all students. Prior to coming to ASU, Brent was a cofounder and provost at the Relay Graduate School of Education, where he set the curricular vision for the institution and managed teams focused on curriculum design, institutional research, and programmatic innovation. While at Relay, Brent also founded TeacherSquared, a national center dedicated to increasing collaboration among teacher preparation institutions. Prior to helping launch TeacherSquared and Relay, Brent earned a doctorate from the Harvard Graduate School of Education, served as a founding staff member at IDEA College Prep, and was a National Board certified teacher in secondary science.

Adam Peshek is the senior director of and a senior fellow at Stand Together Trust (STT), where he focuses on education policy. Prior to joining STT, Peshek spent eight years in leadership positions with ExcelinEd, including as managing policy director. In this role, Peshek provided strategic support to state leaders interested in developing and implementing policies that expanded educational options for children. He also served as vice president of advocacy, directing the organization's advocacy efforts with governors, state legislatures and departments of education, and other stakeholders. Peshek has provided testimony to more than a dozen state legislatures, is a frequent commentator on education policy, and was coeditor of the first published volume on ESAs, *Education Savings Accounts: The New Frontier in School Choice*. Peshek earned bachelor's degrees in political science and interdisciplinary social sciences from Florida State University.

Michael Q. McShane is director of national research at EdChoice. He is the author, editor, coauthor, or coeditor of eleven books on education policy, including his most recent with Frederick M. Hess, *Getting Education Right: A Conservative Vision for Improving Early Childhood, K–12, and College*. He is an opinion contributor to *Forbes*, and his analyses and commentary have been published widely in the media, including in *USA Today*, the *Washington Post*, and the *Wall Street Journal*. He has also been featured in education-specific outlets such as *Teachers College Record*, *Education Week*, *Phi Delta Kappan*, and *Education Next*. In addition to authoring numerous white papers, McShane has had academic work published in *Education Finance and Policy*, *The Handbook of Education Politics and Policy*, and the *Journal of School Choice*. A former high school teacher, he earned a PhD in education policy from the University of Arkansas, an MEd from the University of Notre Dame, and a BA in English from St. Louis University.

Corey Mohn is the president and executive director of CAPS Network, empowering high school students to fast-forward into their future through real-world business projects and the development of professional skills. Prior to CAPS, Corey served as director of statewide programs for the Kansas Center for Entrepreneurship. In July 2015, CAPS launched CAPS Network, a consortium of school programs committed to this model of profession-based education. CAPS Network has grown to include one hundred affiliate programs, including over 180 school districts across twenty-three states and four countries.

Joel Rose is a cofounder and CEO of New Classrooms, an independent nonprofit that brings innovative learning products and models to students. Joel has published articles about personalized learning, innovation, and school models in *The Atlantic*, *The 74*, and *Education Next*. He has spoken at numerous convenings, including the Aspen Institute Ideas Festival; NBC's Education Nation; and the annual conferences for the American Federation of Teachers, National School Boards Association, and National Association of Independent Schools. Joel holds a BA in political science from Tufts University and a JD from the University of Miami School of Law, and he is a Pahara-Aspen education fellow at the Aspen Institute.

Arthur VanderVeen has spent two decades leading organizations that seek to improve learning through assessment, technology, and data. He is founder and CEO of New Meridian, a nonprofit organization that helps states develop better assessments that focus on the skills that matter most for students' future success: critical thinking, reasoning, research, and communication. Previously, Arthur served in several roles with the New York City Department of Education, including chief of innovation and executive director of assessments. He has also worked at Compass Learning and the College Board. Arthur has a PhD in English from the University of Texas at Austin, a Master of Divinity from Princeton Theological Seminary, and a BA from Colorado College.

Larry Berger is the CEO of Amplify, the education company he cofounded as Wireless Generation in 2001. He has led the invention of mobile software to help early reading teachers and next-generation English, math, and science curricula for elementary and middle schools. Larry was a White House fellow working on educational technology at NASA. He was also a Pahara-Aspen education fellow. Larry has published numerous articles on education technology and the use of handheld computing to support diagnostic instruction. He is also the coauthor of *I Will Sing Life*, a book about the poetry writing program he developed and taught for children with serious illnesses. In addition to the Academy of American Poets, he serves on the boards of directors of *Lapham's Quarterly*, the Institute for Sustained Attention, and Touch Press. Larry holds a BA from Yale and was a Rhodes Scholar at Oxford University.

Alexandra Walsh is chief product officer at Amplify. As chief product officer, Alexandra develops, leads, and implements a strategic vision that delivers product coherence and common platform excellence across Amplify's math, literacy, and science product suites. Previously, she was senior vice president and general manager of English language arts (ELA) curriculum, leading the ELA business and overseeing product development on the company's curriculum platform. Prior to Amplify, Alexandra was at the Bridgespan Group, where she provided strategic advisory services to social sector leaders on a range of issues, including education, child welfare, and government effectiveness. She started her career with Teach For America as a high school biology teacher in Louisiana.

Index